PANZER II
vs
7TP

Poland 1939

DAVID R. HIGGINS

First published in Great Britain in 2015 by Osprey Publishing,
PO Box 883, Oxford, OX1 9PL, UK
PO Box 3985, New York, NY 10185-3985, USA
E-mail: info@ospreypublishing.com

Osprey Publishing, part of Bloomsbury Publishing Plc

A CIP catalogue record for this book is available from the British Library

Print ISBN: 978 1 4728 0881 3
PDF ebook ISBN: 978 1 4728 0882 0
ePub ebook ISBN: 978 1 4728 0883 7

Index by Mark Swift
Typeset in ITC Conduit and Adobe Garamond
Maps by bounford.com
Originated by PDQ Media, Bungay, UK
Printed in China through Worldprint Ltd

15 16 17 18 19   10 9 8 7 6 5 4 3 2 1

Osprey Publishing is supporting the Woodland Trust, the UK's leading woodland conservation charity, by funding the dedication of trees.

www.ospreypublishing.com

I would like to thank the following individuals for their kind support without which this book, and my other military history endeavours, might not have been possible: Joseph Miranda, editor-in-chief, *Strategy & Tactics* magazine; Colonel (ret.) Jerry D. Morelock PhD, editor-in-chief, *Armchair General* magazine; Jari Saurio, Curator, The Parola Armour Museum, Finland; Christian Ankerstjerne; Valentinas Kabasinskas; Artur Popiołek; Vasily Diounov (beutepanzer.ru); Sergey Ryijov; Dariusz Antonkiewicz; and my editor Nick Reynolds. Any errors or omissions in this work were certainly unintended, and I alone bear responsibility for them.

Author's note

Army groups/fronts, armies, corps, and divisions employ consistent, but respectively different numbering conventions in this book. Some examples are: Łódź Army (spelled out); XVI. Armeekorps (mot.) (roman numerals); and 28th Infantry Division (Arabic numerals). German unit names are given in the original language, but abbreviated (e.g. Aufklärungs-Abteilung (mot.) 7 is shown as AufklAbt (mot.) 7), while Polish unit names are given in English, with light-tank battalions abbreviated as 'LTB' and independent light-tank companies as 'LTC'.

Editor's note

For ease of comparison please refer to the following conversion table:

1km = 0.62 miles
1m = 1.09yd
1m = 3.28ft
1m = 39.37in
1cm = 0.39in
1mm = 0.04in
1kg = 2.20lb
1g = 0.04oz

Imperial War Museum collections

Many of the photos in this book come from the Imperial War Museum's huge collections which cover all aspects of conflict involving Britain and the Commonwealth since the start of the twentieth century. These rich resources are available online to search, browse and buy at www.iwmcollections.org.uk. In addition to Collections Online, you can visit the Visitor Rooms where you can explore over 8 million photographs, thousands of hours of moving images, the largest sound archive of its kind in the world, thousands of diaries and letters written by people in wartime, and a huge reference library. To make an appointment, call (020) 7416 5320, or e-mail mail@iwm.org.uk
Imperial War Museum www.iwm.org.uk

Comparative officer ranks

Polish	German	British
Marszałek Polski	*Generalfeldmarschall*	field marshal
n/a	*Generaloberst*	general
Generał broni	*General der Panzertruppe*, etc.	lieutenant-general
Generał dywizji	*Generalleutnant*	major-general
Generał brygady	*Generalmajor*	brigadier
Pułkownik	*Oberst*	colonel
Podpułkownik	*Oberstleutnant*	lieutenant-colonel
Major	*Major*	major
Kapitan	*Hauptmann*	captain
Porucznik	*Oberleutnant*	1st lieutenant
Podporucznik	*Leutnant*	2nd lieutenant

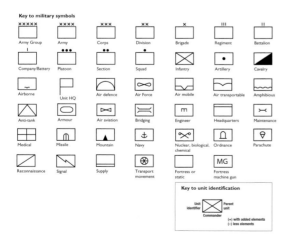

Key to military symbols

Army Group · Army · Corps · Division · Brigade · Regiment · Battalion
Company/Battery · Platoon · Section · Squad · Infantry · Artillery · Cavalry
Airborne · Unit HQ · Air defence · Air Force · Air mobile · Air transportable · Amphibious
Anti-tank · Armour · Air aviation · Bridging · Engineer · Headquarters · Maintenance
Medical · Missile · Mountain · Navy · Nuclear, biological, chemical · Ordnance · Parachute
Reconnaissance · Signal · Supply · Transport movement · Fortress or static · Fortress machine gun

Key to unit identification

Unit identifier · Parent unit · Commander
(+) with added elements
(−) less elements

CONTENTS

INTRODUCTION

As with most conflicts, during the German invasion of Poland in 1939, both participants were forced to employ what military assets were available, rather than those desired. Concerning tanks, Germany's inability to produce sufficient numbers of purpose-built PzKpfw (*Panzerkampfwagen*, or 'armoured fighting vehicle') III and IV combat vehicles meant the lighter, much more numerous PzKpfw II was thrust into the role. For Poland, an equally 'light', but more suitable 7TP (*siedmiotonowy polski*, or '7-tonne Polish') could be fielded, but not in quantities needed to greatly affect the larger battlefield. Although these two armoured fighting vehicles (AFVs) were created as light vehicles, with similar intended battlefield roles, the doctrinal and organizational framework in which each operated represented very different military philosophies and would help to shape the evolution of tank warfare throughout World War II.

On 31 August 1939, German security personnel and convicts dressed in Polish Army uniforms conducted an 'attack' on a radio station near the German–Polish border at Gleiwitz. Having burst into the facility to broadcast a patriotic announcement in Polish and fire a few dramatic rounds before leaving, the overseers killed their unwilling cohorts, and left their bodies as 'evidence' of Polish provocation. A subsequent German radio broadcast railed against the unprovoked attack on the Reich, as a justification for war. At 0434hrs on 1 September, German Ju 87B-2 dive-bombers unsuccessfully targeted the detonators and wiring that Polish engineers would use to destroy the rail and road bridges over the Wisła River at Tczew to prevent their intact capture. Some ten minutes later, the Jutland-era German battleship, *Schleswig-Holstein*, fired into the port city of Danzig/Gdańsk roughly 30km to the north, signalling the official start of the campaign, and potentially a wider European war. German ground and tactical air forces followed up by crossing the border in what was essentially a large double envelopment designed to converge on Warsaw and its

1.2 million citizens, and points further east along the Bug River, and the pre-determined demarcation line with the Soviets. The recently signed Russo-German Pact, which secretly identified their respective zones of control over bordering territories, allocated eastern Poland to Stalin's control.

The spearhead formation of Nazi Germany's 10. Armee, General der Kavallerie Erich Hoepner's XVI. Armeekorps (mot.) was tasked with defeating Poland's Łódź Army; the German corps was then to secure crossings over the Wisła River, some 300km to the north-east, and strike Warsaw. At 0500hrs on 1 September 1939, 4. Panzer-Division, with 324 tanks and 101 other assorted AFVs, set off from Grunsruh towards the three hamlets of Mokra, on what promised to be a clear, warm day. Meanwhile, 1. Panzer-Division pushed towards Kłobuck. Covering the corps' right flank, 14. Infanterie-Division advanced towards Częstochowa, with 31. Infanterie-Division as corps reserve. Awaiting the German onslaught along an extended front, Colonel (qual.) Julian Filipowicz established most of his Wołyńska Cavalry Brigade along the crescent-shaped wooded area encompassing the three Mokra villages north of Kłobuck. Although such Polish formations used horses for manoeuvre, they fought as infantry that was reinforced with towed weapons that could deliver considerable firepower.

The ensuing battle of Mokra would demonstrate to the world the power of the *Blitzkrieg*, with the PzKpfw II at the forefront of the German drive to Warsaw. The relatively easy German advance ended at around 0800hrs, as 4. Panzer-Division's spearheads advanced beyond Krzepice; Polish soldiers that were assumed to have been

With the fighting in central Poland winding down, Hitler presided over an 8. Armee victory parade in the recently captured enemy capital on 5 October 1939. Although PzKpfw I Ausf B, such as these, were ill-suited for direct combat, necessity often dictated otherwise; including the fight for Warsaw. Soon to gain fame commanding 7. Panzer-Division in the West, Generalmajor Erwin Rommel – a distant cousin of Łódź Army's commander, Major General Juliusz Rómmel – stands next to Hitler as head of the Führerbegleithauptquartier (Führer Escort Headquarters) having provided security for the event. (© IWM COL 149)

These dual-turret 7TPs are pictured during a pre-war public demonstration. (John Phillips/ The LIFE Picture Collection/Getty Images)

killed or incapacitated, suddenly opened fire, inflicting heavy casualties that forced the Germans back. In advance of a renewed offensive push, elements of 4. Panzer-Division pushed Polish cavalry back into the Mokra Woods at around 1000hrs. As German tanks manoeuvred to exploit the situation, the 1920s-era Armoured Train 53 suddenly emerged from the woods to lob 75mm rounds into their midst, as Armoured Train 52 remained out of sight further behind. In the resulting panic and chaos, defending cavalry covering the Polish right managed slowly to extricate itself eastwards.

At 1300hrs, the German main attack on Mokra began, using 100 tanks that spread through the three hamlets, only to have Armoured Train 53 keep them at bay. With Wołyńska Cavalry Brigade largely spent, at 1600hrs, tankettes of Poland's 21st Armoured Troop came out of reserve to engage several German AFVs. Polish 37mm antitank guns, backed by artillery, again rebuffed the German advance; in one instance, panicked German rear-echelon supply personnel thought they would be overrun, and only direct intervention of Generalmajor Georg-Hans Reinhardt, 4. Panzer-Division's commander, stopped them. By day's end the Polish defenders had inflicted considerable casualties in men and matériel, but with other sectors having given way Wołyńska Cavalry Brigade finally withdrew that night. German spearheads soon followed to maintain the advance with minimal interruption, and open the route to Piotrków.

With Wołyńska Cavalry Brigade, and its flanking formations, under increasing pressure to conduct an effective, elastic defence, Poland's Prusy Army was forced to allocate formations piecemeal to the fight to maintain a stable front line. On 27 August, Poland's 2nd Light Tank Battalion (2nd LTB) had begun accepting reservists and equipment, and organizing, as part of its mobilization in Żurawica near Przemyśl far to the east. As some single-turret 7TPs only had machine guns as they awaited their 37mm guns to be fitted, it was 29 August before the complete formation was combat-ready. In excellent spirits and physical condition, all assembled took the oath before leaving. At 0400hrs on 30 August the battalion had boarded two trains for a circuitous, 900km route through Lwów, Kowel, Brześć, Siedlce, Warsaw, Sochaczew and finally the Bednary station just shy of Łowicz on 1 September. As war had commenced in the interim, on arrival at 1700hrs the unit's commander, Major Edmund Karpow, ordered it to move 4km south to establish positions in a wooded area near Nieborów for concealment. Having transitioned to front-line duty, 2nd LTB was subsequently subordinated to Major-General Juliusz Rómmel's Lódź Army where it was to defend the border south-west of Warsaw against 8. Armee and 10. Armee.

Meanwhile, having been redirected from the Polish Corridor fight, Major Adam Kubin's 1st LTB arrived at Słotwiny station near Koluszki and established positions in the forests near Tomaszów Mazowiecki, roughly halfway between the German border and Warsaw. Although both light-tank battalions had now been allocated to Prusy Army, senior commanders struggled with how best to apply these armoured elements. While 2nd LTB stumbled southwards to establish positions near Piotrków, Major Adam Kubin's tankers were ordered to patrol its new operational area to little effect, save expending precious fuel. It would be Monday 4 September 1939 before the two sides' tanks clashed in earnest, near Wola Krzysztoporska in the Góry Borowskie Hills, and the bloody encounter would be momentous for both sides.

Monday 25 September 1939: German troops advance on the outskirts of Warsaw behind the dubious cover afforded by a PzKpfw II. Aggressively deployed but poorly handled, German tanks like this one would receive a bloody rebuff in the streets of the Polish capital. Initially told they would be perticipating in military exercises lasting several weeks, once activated Germany's soldiers were not excited about going to war in September 1939, as had been nearly universal in 1914; rather they saw it as their job and duty, and something for which they were trained. Considering the vitriolic rhetoric from both sides, they had little reason to doubt the authenticity of the 'pre-emptive' Gleiwitz Incident, and were supportive of the Polish campaign as a way to restore German honour. (Popperfoto/Getty Images)

CHRONOLOGY

1926

2 October   The Germans and Soviets reach agreement to establish Panzerschule Kama.

1933

19 January   PZInż is contracted to build the first two 7TPs.

24 June   The 7TP's design phase is completed.

1 November   Oswald Lutz organizes Nazi Germany's first tank formation, Kraftfahrlehrkommando Zossen.

1934

July   Germany's Waffenamt orders the development of a 9-tonne tank, with a 2cm automatic cannon.

Early August   The first 7TP prototype, 'Dragon', is produced.

1935

Krupp AG, MAN, Henschel & Sohn AG and Daimler-Benz AG submit prototypes of the LaS 100.

18 March   Series 1 7TP production is ordered.

15 October   1. Panzer-Division is formed.

1937

March   The Polish authorities place their first order for the 37mm wz.37 L/45 cannon.

1938

June   First PzKpfw II Ausf C is produced.

10 November   4. Panzer-Division is formed.

1939

1 September   The battle of Mokra.

2 September   The battle of Borowa Góra begins as elements of 1. Panzer-Division cross the Warta River at Gidle.

4 September   7TPs of 1/2nd LTB inflict disproportionate losses on PzKpfw I and PzKpfw II of 1. Panzer-Division's vanguard near Wola Krzysztoporska.

5 September   Two companies of 2nd LTB try unsuccessfully to hamper 1. Panzer-Division's advance on Piotrków.

A PzKpfw II leading a pair of PzKpfw I, a second PzKpfw II and, bringing up the rear, two PzBefh I command tanks. With an enclosed superstructure instead of a turret, these converted PzKpfw I tanks provided room for maps, and the necessary accoutrements to co-ordinate actions. In some cases, the PzKpfw III was similarly reconfigured as a command version. (NARA)

6 September	Having encircled Piotrków, 1. Panzer-Division and 4. Panzer-Division push on Tomaszów Mazowiecki.
7 September	With the Polish government having abandoned Warsaw, 1st LTB withdraws to Inowłódz en route to defend the Polish capital.
8 September	PzKpfw II tanks of PzRgt 35 engage 7TPs of 2nd LTB at Narutowicza Square on the outskirts of Warsaw.
9 September	Warsaw Defence Commands are created from 7TPs that had been undergoing trials.
10 September	7TPs of 2nd LTB ambush PzKpfw II tanks of PzRgt 36 near Warsaw Cemetery, on the Polish capital's south-western edge.
11 September	Worn down from combat and movement, 2nd LTB is disbanded, one day after 1st LTB is disbanded.
12 September	British and French staffs meet at Abbeville, France, and decide not to attack Germany's weakened Western Front.
14 September	Elements of 4. Panzer-Division turn westwards to help block a Polish break-out from the Bzura Pocket.

A 7TP repurposed by the Germans, as denoted by the crudely painted *Balkenkreuz*. The open turret rear housed a radio (if available). The *Kradmantel* (rubberized overcoat) worn by the soldier at left indicates he is a motorcyclist. (Courtesy Sergey Ryijov, beutepanzer.ru (Vasily Diounov))

17 September	The Soviets invade eastern Poland.
6 October	The Polish campaign ends.

1940

April	PzKpfw II Ausf C production ceases.

A handful of PzKpfw I and PzKpfw II varieties were adapted to provide the *Pioniere* with the capability to deploy a bridge while under fire. Here, *Pionier* tanks of 1. Panzer-Division – including the lead PzKpfw II Ausf C, and a second PzKpfw II *Brückenleger* further back – are pictured during the 1940 campaign in France and the Low Countries. Also visible are two PzKpfw I Ausf B tanks that have been converted into the Ladungsleger I variant, with a gantry for deploying a 50kg demolition charge. (NARA)

DESIGN AND DEVELOPMENT

ARMOUR AFTER WORLD WAR I

Germany's PzKpfw II and Poland's 7TP both owed their origins to the revolution in warfare brought about by the seismic events of World War I. These AFVs would be conceived, refined and eventually deployed in combat according to underlying assumptions about the conduct of land warfare held by senior commanders in both countries, some of whom had achieved their standing owing to reasons other than military merit, in an environment where overly conservative mindsets sometimes precluded flexibility of action and learning from mistakes. These beliefs would combine with the economic realities of the interwar era to shape the development of the two designs in the years before 1939.

The widespread use of tanks by the Entente Powers contributed significantly to the defeat of the Central Powers on World War I's Western Front, and during the 1920s and 1930s all the former belligerents would struggle to determine how best to fund tank development, and to organize their armoured forces for use in a future conflict. Tanks had been developed to address a particular problem – the reintroduction of operational movement to the Western Front with its trenches, massed artillery, barbed wire and machine guns. Senior commanders often believed tanks to be expensive, mechanically unreliable and lacking in the speed and endurance necessary to inflict a decisive strike to the enemy. Constrained by greatly reduced peacetime budgets, and a widespread consensus that the tank concept had outlived its usefulness – due in large

measure to improvements in anti-tank technology – the path to creating modern armoured forces and commensurate doctrine was fraught with controversy and disagreement.

Considering Britain and France's extensive experience producing and maintaining armoured vehicles, other nations – Poland and Germany among them – sought to adopt or adapt their respective doctrines for their own fledgling tank forces. A variety of designs were envisaged, reflecting the current make-up of the armed forces of each country. To complement the differing speeds and capabilities of both the infantry and cavalry, heavily armed and armoured vehicles would work with the former to engage bunkers and built-up positions to affect a penetration, while lighter, more manoeuvrable designs were to operate in reconnaissance and pursuit roles. Some, though, challenged these assumptions by promoting the tank as a core component in a new kind of warfare, and not simply a mechanized extension of the horse. Although many conventional German commanders sought to parcel AFVs along a front, a select cadre of senior officers, such as Hans von Seeckt, Oswald Lutz and Heinz Guderian, envisaged an alternative approach based largely upon the conclusions of a handful of British armour theorists, including B.H. Liddell Hart, Giffard Martel and J.F.C. Fuller, who promoted concentrated, self-supporting, all-arms formations built around the tank that would undertake a series of offensives to outmanoeuvre and destroy a modern adversary. In the same vein, Soviet commanders such as Mikhail Tukhachevsky believed such forces could exploit Eastern Europe's largely rural, open terrain by conducting deep, far-ranging operations into an enemy's rear areas to target command and control and logistics, and sow confusion – tactics that were at odds with official Soviet ideas involving mass and numbers. Hoping to avoid repeating a war on multiple

A Renault FT tank in the Rhineland in 1919. During World War I, the British and French had both experimented with a variety of configurations; the latter arguably fielded the most successful tank, as evidenced by its serving as the basis for future designs. While other AFVs of World War I featured a relatively open interior, negligible suspension, numerous cannon and machine guns, and large crews that were directly exposed to engine exhaust, noise and heat, the French Renault FT incorporated heavy springs for a smoother ride and a compartmentalized chassis that physically separated the two-man crew from a rear-mounted engine. It also introduced a single, rotating turret positioned atop the vehicle that improved the commander's view, and allowed the primary armament a better range of motion. (Three Lions/Getty Images)

Białystok, early 1920s: mounted and motorized elements of Poland's armed forces participate in the annual celebration of Polish independence. The vital role played by the Polish cavalry in the victorious war against the Soviet Union meant that the mounted arm remained disproportionately important in terms of manpower and funding, to the detriment of Poland's nascent armoured forces. (FORUM/Polish Photography Agency)

fronts which would steadily erode Germany's fighting capability, its farsighted officers placed emphasis on maintaining a rapid battlefield tempo to win a campaign quickly, freeing armoured and motorized forces for commitment elsewhere.

Although it had fielded AFVs during World War I, Germany had preferred to compensate for its inferior numbers and resources by adopting specialist, small-unit infiltration tactics to restore operational movement. In the 1920s and 1930s many senior German officers would see the value in evolving these techniques to suit armoured and motorized formations possessing the necessary strength, endurance and composition to promote a rapid battlefield tempo, and the flexibility to adapt to fluid combat situations. With another European war in the offing in 1939, lingering uncertainty about armour's battlefield validity would soon be settled.

PzKpfw II

ORIGINS

In the form of the Versailles Treaty, the victorious Entente Powers imposed a huge burden of war debt upon Germany, and sought to eliminate its warmaking capability for the foreseeable future by limiting the country's military to a 100,000-man force – the Reichswehr, led by Generaloberst Hans von Seeckt. Useful for little more than internal and border security, the Reichswehr was prohibited from possessing or producing a variety of modern weapon systems, including AFVs. In an effort to circumvent these measures, the German authorities resorted to subterfuge to evade foreign inspectors and quietly prepare for eventual rearmament. To supplement the Reichswehr's limited power, the recently abolished, but secretly retained Großer Generalstab ('Greater General Staff') – rechristened the Truppenamt ('Troop Office') – along with wealthy industrialists and other conservative/nationalist groups, helped fund, train and equip the numerous *Freikorps* – paramilitary veteran organizations –

across the country. Military and industry elements also quietly contracted with suitable foreign-located firms to produce contraband. In particular, the Swedish firm Firman Petterson & Ohlsen – known as AB Landsverk from 1928 – was from 1925 61 per cent owned by the German company Gutehoffnungshütte Actienverein für Bergbau und Hüttenbetrieb, Sterkrade (GHH), which had also acquired the German engineering and manufacturing giant Maschinenfabrik Augsburg-Nürnberg AG (MAN) in 1921. This covert activity provided Germany with an outlet for producing tanks beyond the watchful eyes of their former adversaries. Although fledgling, under Seeckt's determined leadership, a German *Panzerwaffe* (armoured force) would soon be in the offing.

As part of the 1922 German–Soviet Rapallo Treaty, in which both former adversaries abandoned all territorial and financial claims on the other, secret agreements led to the establishment of several training and testing facilities, including aircraft (Lipetsk, 1925), chemical weapons (Prichernavskaya, 1926) and armour (Kazan, 1926). These were intended to permit mutual instruction and the testing of new tactics, weapons and vehicles, with funding hidden from Germany's official state budget. The armour facility, under the German cover name Panzertruppenschule Kama (for the nearby city of Kazan and its first Director, Oberstleutnant aD Wilhelm Malbrandt) had Reichsheer officers teach emerging German military doctrine to their own officers alongside their Soviet opposite numbers – many of whom would become bitter enemies in 1941.

With the Kama training programme completed in early 1929, it was placed under the control of the Soviet Union's NKVD (Ministry of State Security). Between 1926 and 1933, Friedrich Krupp AG, Rheinmetall-Borsig AG and Daimler-Benz AG used the facility to test new tank prototypes, including a 8,700kg *Kleintraktor* (later *Leichttraktor*) and what were intended to be 'heavy' *Großtraktor* designs of between 15,000kg and 19,320kg. Company engineers at Kazan also experimented with AFV components, with perhaps the most important being the incorporation of two-way radios that greatly facilitated the tactical communication among vehicles and formations, and with command. In return, the Soviets received valuable engineering and manufacturing expertise for their own armour programme, although they remained cautious about too much collaboration, considering their old enemy funded and controlled the facility's operation. After Kama, German prototypes were often sent to Heereszeugamt (Army Ordnance Supply Office) Spandau for overhaul. Additional testing occurred in Wustrow, followed by large unit manoeuvres at Truppenübungsplatz (Troop Training Grounds) Münster, and gunnery training at the newly established Truppenübungsplatz Putlos, along the Baltic Sea.

One unintended benefit of Germany's post-war situation was that unlike the victors, the Germans were not saddled with an abundance of ageing surplus equipment that retarded the development of newer tank designs and ideas. Appointed Inspekteur der Verkehrstruppen (Inspector of Motor Transport) in 1931, Generalmajor Oswald Lutz, along with his chief of staff, Oberstleutnant Heinz Guderian, aggressively orchestrated Germany's covert rearmament. These two men saw a need for a small, introductory tank

Adolf Hitler, Nazi Germany's *Führer*, confers with Generaloberst von Seeckt in autumn 1936. Reflecting the Reichswehr's mindset, Seeckt viewed Poland as Germany's greatest threat, based upon that country's vitriolic rhetoric and actions. These included violence against ethnic Germans, and 'land reforms' that forced thousands to flee their ancestral homes east of the Oder River between 1919 and 1921. While Seeckt intended to address the production, organizing, fielding and deployment of military assets, his focus on the tank translated into an emphasis on developing technologies such as radio communications, and the improvement of vehicle speeds and operational ranges in order to implement the developing offensive doctrine. Accordingly, he looked to the Soviet Union, which had similarly lost territory recently to the newly created country. With Poland eliminated, the combined might of Germany and the Soviet Union promised to be sufficient to dominate the remainder of Europe. (Imagno/Getty Images)

13

Tuesday 19 September 1939: a PzKpfw III Ausf D (note the rear idler wheel from an earlier model) negotiates a temporary bridge, while other German armour moves past in the background. With Adolf Hitler's rise to power, Germany's quiet national rearmament increased in importance and exposure. Although the government avoided providing subsidies for equipment and machinery, it did for development costs. Development of the PzKpfw III and PzKpfw IV only began in 1936; the PzKpfw III Ausf E would be the first true production variant of the former, but between December 1938 and October 1939 only 96 would be made, while only 134 PzKpfw IV Ausf C fire-support tanks would be produced between September 1938 and August 1939. To make up for this shortfall, and flesh out armored formations with sufficient vehicles, the light PzKpfw II was thrust from its training role into front-line combat operations. Although the light tank was unsuited for such tasks, and suffered accordingly, their numbers, and support from mechanized, motorized and aerial assets, promoted a rapid German advance against an increasingly fragmented enemy defence. (© Berliner Verlag/Archiv/dpa/Corbis)

with which to conduct training, and to acclimatize locomotive, steel and other industries to developing AFVs. Accordingly, in 1932 Friedrich Krupp AG, Rheinmetall-Borsig AG, MAN and Daimler-Benz AG received orders to develop a prototype for what was innocuously designated a *Landwirtschaftlicher Schlepper* ('agricultural tractor'). With Krupp's Landswerk Krupp A (LKA) solution chosen for being cheap and quick to produce, field testing of what would become the PzKpfw I was undertaken at the Kummersdorf Proving Grounds in mid-1933. Following refinement, the German authorities made the unorthodox choice to produce components and conduct tank assembly at multiple factories, in order to broaden expertise related to AFV manufacturing.

On 1 November 1933 the first German tank unit was formed. Kraftfahrlehrkommando (Motor Transport Training Command) Zossen consisted of a skeleton company of 14 tractors. On 16 July 1934 the Heereswaffenamt (Army Ordnance Office) requested designs for what was to be a better-armed supplement to the small PzKpfw I, just coming off the assembly lines. The proposed LaS 100 (Landwirtschaftlicher Schlepper 100) was to weigh 9,800kg and possess a 2cm automatic cannon capable of firing both armour-piercing and high-explosive projectiles. Widely available and compact, this 2cm gun was suitable for testing a vehicle the size of the LaS 100, and its high rate of fire would be beneficial during reconnaissance or peripheral combat duties. Intended to engage in combat, as part of the war of manoeuvre, the vehicle was not designed for a stand-up fight against enemy armour, but that would be the role it had to fill in 1939.

DEVELOPMENT AND PRODUCTION

This new AFV was variously designated the '2cm MG Panzerwagen' and the 'VK 622' (*Versuchkraftfahrzeug*, or 'test vehicle'). Although Krupp was the first of several firms to submit prototype solutions, their 'LKA 1' derivative, designated 'LKA 2', was not chosen. Instead, in early 1935 MAN was tasked with developing the new vehicle's chassis, while Daimler-Benz AG focused on the superstructure and turret. With the design having proven itself at Kummersdorf, to reduce development and production times and increase manufacturing experience, the other contenders were to provide major components, including Henschel & Sohn AG (chassis only); Wegmann; Alkett; Mühlenbau & Industrie Aktiengesellschaft (MIAG); Fahrzeug & Motorenbau GmbH (FAMO); and Krupp.

Starting in October 1935, the prototype stage began with three vehicle iterations as part of the 1/LaS 100 series; emphasis was placed on finding an optimal chassis and other components, balanced against estimated manufacturing time and cost, ease of maintenance and durability. The 25 Ausf a/1 and 25 Ausf a/2 models had very minor differences, with the 25 Ausf a/3 tanks possessing a larger engine and improved suspension; all had six road wheels and a horizontal brace as on the PzKpfw I, and three return rollers per side.

To address the understrength 97kW Maybach engine, during February and March 1937 a larger 103kW motor was incorporated into what was designated the Ausf b (2/LaS 100), with 100 examples produced. This necessitated a new reduction gear to increase driveshaft-produced torque, and stronger vehicle mountings to support its slight weight increase to about 8,900kg. All four iterations totalled 175 vehicles, augmented by some 31 subsequent Ausf c tanks; as per Hitler's desire to expand Germany's armoured forces rapidly, many of these prototypes were issued to Panzer units in early 1936 to supplement fielded PzKpfw I tanks. Roughly 44 additional Ausf c tanks, designated 3/LaS 100, incorporated five larger, independently sprung road wheels, and an additional fourth return roller; intended to increase mobility and aid maintenance, this configuration was retained into production. As volume and manufacturing experience increased, development costs decreased by some 28 per cent since prototype development commenced.

With the LaS 100 prototypes having proved the design, in July 1937 the vehicle entered production as the Ausf A, with a handful of enhancements over the Ausf c; 210 were produced. The Ausf B (384 built from December 1937) and Ausf C (produced from June 1938) followed, with the latter receiving the designation PzKpfw II. The PzKpfw II Ausf C was authorized chassis numbers 26001–27000, although after six series runs only 364 Ausf C tanks had been built when production ended in April 1940. By this time the PzKpfw II Ausf C had been shown to be generally outclassed in combat; around 70 per cent of those available would be up-armoured between the end of the Polish campaign and the beginning of the fighting in France and the Low Countries.

Intended for the *leichte Divisionen* – the German Cavalry's chosen armoured formation – the Ausf D and E sported different track configurations, but deviated considerably from the previous PzKpfw II models, having different hulls and Christie suspensions that used torsion bars, which better protected the suspension and permitted a speed increase. With only 43 examples of the former produced, by September 1939 sufficient numbers of these cavalry variants had been produced to equip only one unit, however. Along with several Ausf A, these Ausf E and a handful of Ausf F chassis were eventually converted into flamethrower variants.

A PzKpfw II Ausf A. Following the Polish campaign, Ausf D and later versions would incorporate a low turret cupola and additional frontal armour. The angled piece along the hull was for the antenna, and the glacis carries tow cables. The PzKpfw II's internal layout comprised a port-side forward driving position, where the driver/mechanic sat in a confined space bordered by the hull, forward axle and transmission, with its longitudinal driveshaft. To avoid the driver/mechanic having to move through the turret, an access hatch was provided in the glacis. The position also had two chassis-welded handholds close to where the detachable superstructure was bolted, and two holes bored through the armour above the driver's flap allowed for a binocular periscope when buttoned up. To improve production costs and logistics, German AFVs used two types of vision flaps; a bevelled variety with a viewing slit, and a plain flat plate. To protect the viewer's face the former were backed by detachable, laminated-glass blocks 12mm thick, with a steel version available as needed. (Christian Ankerstjerne)

PzKpfw II Ausf C SPECIFICATIONS

General
Production run: June 1938–April 1940 (22 months)

Vehicles produced: 364

Combat weight: 8,900kg

Suspension: Five quarter-elliptic leaf-spring

Crew: three (commander/gunner, driver, loader/radio operator)

Dimensions
Length: 4.81m

Width: 2.22m

Height: 1.99m

Armour (degrees from vertical)
Glacis (upper / middle / lower): 14.5mm @ 73° / 14.5mm round / 14.5mm @ 64°

Hull face: 14.5mm @ 9°

Hull side: 14.5mm @ 0°

Hull rear (upper / lower): 14.5mm @ 7° / 10mm @ 62°

Hull roof (deck/engine): 14.5mm @ 90° / 10mm @ 82°

Hull bottom: 5mm @ 90

Turret face (front / base): 14.5mm round / 14.5mm @ 16°

Turret side: 14.5mm @ 22°

Turret rear: 14.5mm @ 23°

Turret roof (upper / front): 10mm @ 90° / 10mm @ 76°

Mantlet: 16mm round

Armament
Main gun: 2cm KwK 30 L/55 (180 PzGr 39 and Sprgr 39 in 18 ten-round magazines)

Sight: TZF 4/38 (2.5×)

Elevation: +20° / -9.5°

Secondary: 1 × 7.92mm MG 34 (coaxial) (1,425 rounds in 19 × 75-round magazines)

Main gun rate of fire (cyclic / effective): 280rds/min / 120rds/min

Communications
Internal: Voice tube

External: FuG 5

Motive power
Engine: Maybach HL 62 TR 6-cylinder (water cooled) 6,191cc (petrol)

Power to weight: 103kW (sustained) @ 2,600rpm (11.57kW/tonne)

Transmission: Zahnradfabrik Aphon SSG 46 gearbox; six forward gears, one reverse gear

Fuel capacity: 170l (102l, 68l)

Performance
Ground pressure: 0.62kg/cm²

Speed (maximum / road / cross-country): 40km/h / 25km/h / 15km/h

Operational range (road / cross-country): 190km / 130km

Fuel consumption (road / cross-country): 0.89l/km / 1.35l/km

Fording: 850mm

Step climbing: 420mm

Climbing angle: 30°

Trench crossing: 1.7m

Ground clearance: 340mm

PzKpfw II Ausf C, PzRgt 35

The RAL (Reichsausschuss für Lieferbedingungen, or 'Reich Committee for Terms and Conditions of Sale') paint was provided as paste, which was diluted prior to application. To ensure consistency, specifications were sent to paint suppliers, with details on preparation, after which test specimens had to pass examination and approval, and once at the assembly facilities inspectors used swatches to determine whether the post-application colour matched initial specifications. The PzKpfw II's interior was ivory, *Elfenbein* (RAL 1001), over a red primer, while the exterior sported a two-tone scheme of dark grey, *Dunkelgrau* (RAL 46, later renumbered RAL 7021), as a base coat. Over this, irregular patches of dark brown, *Dunkelbraun* (RAL 45, later renumbered RAL 7017), were spray-painted onto roughly one-third of the surface.

Vehicle identification generally comprised three digits applied to each turret side, indicating the company and platoon to which the tank belonged, and its individual number. *Panzer-Abteilung* command vehicles used prefixed Roman numerals (e.g. 'II01' for II. Abteilung), while regimental varieties used an 'R' (e.g. 'R01'). Initially, a white *Balkenkreuz* was used for nationality identification, but as these were found to be overly visible, crews often subdued them.

4.81m

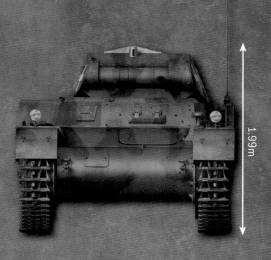

1.99m

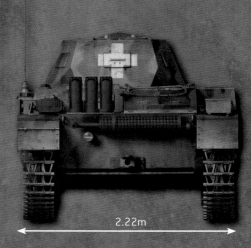

2.22m

7TP

ORIGINS

During the Russo-Polish War (1919–21) tactics retained a Napoleonic flavour, due in large measure to the considerable number of cavalry employed, even though several hundred French military advisors provided the Poles with training and guidance based on lessons learned during World War I. Polish officers tended to be wealthy, aristocratic, and prone to taking risks – a combination their French counterparts had favoured in 1914, and soon tempered. Generals Władysław Sikorski and Józef Piłsudski exemplified such thinking by promoting offensive operations comprising rapid movement and concentration to achieve surprise and a decisive outcome, something not possible while on the defensive. Piłsudski's experience in World War I led him to believe that cavalry was no longer a significant offensive force, and hence he preferred to concentrate on improvements in infantry and artillery. Most also maintained an air of chivalry that was out of place on a modern battlefield. The Poles derided their Soviet adversaries for using *tachanka*, a heavy machine gun mounted on horse-drawn carts to support cavalry operations, but such thinking unnecessarily limited the Poles' options and means of conducting total war.

Although cavalry had been relegated to peripheral operations on the Western Front, in the more open East such forces were critical for rapidly projecting power or providing reconnaissance. Considering their country's geography, the Poles naturally adopted many of their Russian adversaries' battlefield tactics. For all the new technologies developed during the conflict, including poison gas, aircraft and armoured vehicles, the attritional fighting on the Western Front had left many thinking that tanks were a mechanically unreliable novelty that presented a greater danger to their crews than to the enemy. As their rudimentary design made them largely unsuited for the highly mobile operations during the Russo-Polish War, as evidenced with the Renault FT, armoured trains filled the void to provide cavalry support.

The invaluable role played by cavalry during the Russo-Polish War led to a mistaken confidence among military leaders as to the value of cavalry in battle. Many felt that the tank was overrated as a weapon, difficult to manoeuvre and liable to break down in rough terrain. Moreover, fodder for horses was easier to procure than the enormous amounts of petrol required to power tanks. While there were individuals such as Sikorski who recognized the importance of rapid mechanization, there were other considerations. Piłsudski was widely recognized as the 'founder and father of the Polish Army' and insisted on retaining the final say on all military matters. As he grew old and ill it became impossible to draw his attention to fundamental problems in doctrine and armament. There was also the question of Poland's limited financial resources and industrial productive capacity. In 1939, the cost of equipping an entire armoured division exceeded the total annual budget for the entire Polish Army. Despite the fact that Poland spent a sizeable portion of its domestic product on the military, its defence expenditure between 1935 and 1939 sadly amounted to only one thirtieth that of Germany's.

With the Versailles Treaty having granted Poland its independence in June 1919, the country's military initially relied on 120 small French Renault FT derivatives. Over the next decade, additional vehicles were imported to provide a modicum of an armoured force, which by 1931 totalled some 174 tanks – enough for three mixed

The Polish 7TP's precursor, the Vickers E (dual-turret version shown), shared many components with the Polish tank, including suspension, hull and superstructure. Although the 7TP had slightly thicker armour than its Vickers predecessor, it still possessed shortcomings, such as the vertical plate between the turret and driver's hatch, which weakened frontal armour due to the difference made by the driver's plate, and the hull's higher sides presented a larger silhouette than the Vickers. The turret's base was reinforced with an armoured strip, as was the top-mounted ventilator. (Public Domain)

armoured regiments. To avoid relying on modernizing ageing foreign designs, Poland soon began domestic production of tiny TK-1 and TK-2 *tankietka* (tankette) prototypes that were modelled on the British Carden-Loyd Mark VI, and although unsuited for direct combat operations they provided manufacturers with experience in AFV development, much like the rationale behind the German PzKpfw I.

As much of World War I's fighting in the East had occurred across partitioned Polish territory, agriculture, industry and the economy were in a very poor state. The authorities struggled to return damaged and destroyed manufacturing to operation, and to organize recently acquired German, Austrian and Russian industrial assets. In an effort towards producing a true turreted AFV, on 14 September 1931 Poland purchased 50 Vickers Mark E light tanks: 16 Model A (single turret), 22 Model B (twin turret), and 12 disassembled to provide parts. The British military had rejected these over suspension concerns, although other countries saw merit in the design. An accompanying licence allowed some of these buyers to produce the design domestically, including the chassis and running gear. With initial deliveries to Poland having begun in 1932, Polish engineers improved many of the 5,400kg vehicle's shortcomings, including an underpowered engine and low armour quality; it was eventually decided to apply the knowledge gained to produce a domestic version of the British vehicle that inherently incorporated these refinements, instead of cobbling them together after production.

DEVELOPMENT AND PRODUCTION

On 19 January 1933 PZInż (Państwowe Zakłady Inżynieryjne, or 'National Engineering Works') issued a contract to build the first two tanks as part of a programme designated VAU-33 (Vickers-Armstrong-Ursus [19]33). The design phase was completed on 24 June, but it took until early August 1934 before the first 7TP prototype, *Smok* ('Dragon'), no. 1595, emerged, with iron boilerplate in lieu of more expensive steel, which was unnecessary at this stage. Between 16 August and 1 September 'Dragon' underwent nearly 1,100km of comparative field trials, where it demonstrated good mobility, but as

7TP SPECIFICATIONS

General

Production run: 1935–August 1939

Vehicles produced: 139

Combat weight: 9,900kg

Suspension: Leaf-sprung bogies

Crew: Three (commander, gunner, driver/mechanic)

Dimensions

Length: 4.6m

Width: 2.4m

Height: 2.3m

Armour (degrees from vertical)

Glacis (upper starboard / upper port / lower): 17mm @ 27° / 17mm @ 0°/ 17mm @ 80°

Hull face: 14.5mm @ 37°

Hull side: 13mm @ 0°

Hull rear (upper / lower): 5mm @ 30° / 10mm @ 79°

Hull roof (deck / engine): 10mm @ 90° / 10mm @ 90°

Hull bottom: 9.5mm @ 90°

Turret face: 14.5mm @ 0°

Turret side (starboard / port): 15mm @ 15° / 15mm @ 10°

Turret rear: 15mm @ 10°

Turret roof (front / middle / rear): 10mm @ 74° / 10mm @ 90° / 10mm @ 83°

Mantlet (main / MG): 10mm @ 0° / 8mm @ 0°

Armament

Main gun: 37mm Bofors wz.37 L/45 (80 AP, APHE and HE)

Sight: wz.37 CA (1.4×)

Elevation: +20° / -10° (manual)

Secondary: 1 × 7.92mm Ckm wz.30 MG (coaxial) (3,960 rounds in 12 × 330-round fabric belts)

Main gun rate of fire: 10rds/min

Communications

Internal: Voice

External: N2/C or RKBc (command vehicles)

Motive power

Engine: PZInż.235 (Saurer VBLDb) inverted inline six-cylinder (water cooled) four-stroke direct injection (diesel) 8,550cm³ displacement

Power to weight: 82kW (sustained)@1,800rpm (8.28kW/tonne)

Transmission: Dry multidisc gearbox; four forward gears, one reverse gear

Fuel capacity: 110l + 20l reserve

Performance

Ground pressure: 0.60kg/cm²

Speed (road / cross-country): 37km/h / 32km/h

Operational range (road / cross-country): 160km / 130km

Fuel consumption (road / cross-country): 0.81l/km / 1l/km

Fording: 1m

Step climbing: 750mm

Climbing angle: 36°

Trench crossing: 1.8m

Ground clearance: 381mm

7TP, 2nd LIGHT TANK BATTALION

The 7TP sported several camouflage schemes consisting of brown, sand and olive green, although dark grey was occasionally used, as with 2/2nd LTB. 'Horizontal' and 'chequerboard' patterns were also common. Insignia and markings were normally removed in combat conditions, but in peacetime, Polish reconnaissance and light tanks used geometric tactical symbols to identify command and unit vehicles. A white circle, white triangle and red triangle respectively signified 1st Platoon, 2nd Platoon and 3rd Platoon, while a vertical red bar or surrounding white triangle denoted the commander. A white triangle, within a red circle in a white square represented the company commander. Individual vehicles in 1st LTB were given white numbers on the forward hull, with some having white vertical bars — one bar indicating 1st Platoon, two, 2nd Platoon, and three, 3rd Platoon — with command vehicles having a horizontal white stripe underneath. Such designations were also used on other company vehicles. Symbols were occasionally applied to the turrets, including a bison in a white, blue or gold circle, or a leaping white lynx.

4.6m

2.3m

2.4m

its road speed proved slower than expected its cooling system was improved and the suspension was strengthened. A second prototype, *Słoń* ('Elephant'), no. 1596, was allocated to CWBrPanc (Centrum Wyszkolenia Broni Pancernych, or 'Armoured Weapons Training Centre') on 13 August 1935.

In late 1934 the Warsaw-based WIBI (Wojskowy Instytut Badań Inżynierii, or 'Military Institute of Engineering Research') initiated work on the improved design, in co-operation with with PZInż. On behalf of WIBI, under engineer Antoni Fabrykowski, the 7TP ('7-tonne Polish') was to feature a more powerful engine, less weight and an electric starter. Due to limited numbers of suitable petrol engines, the diesel VBLDb (designated the PZInż 235 by the Poles) was incorporated; this necessitated increasing the vehicle's size, springs and suspension, extending its wheel bearing, and modifying the cooling system.

Satisfied with the testing and evaluation of 'Dragon', on 18 March 1935 the Dowództwo Broni Pancernych Ministerstwa Spraw Wojskowych (Ministry of Military Affairs, Armoured Command) ordered Series 1 production of 22 of the 7TP dual-turret variant under the designation 'No. 665/34-35 Armoured', including six for training. Just four examples were produced that year, with the remainder completed in 1936. Although a 7.92mm Ckm wz.30 machine gun was mounted in each, more powerful configurations were considered, including having one of the turrets possess a 13.2mm Browning wz.30 machine gun or a 37mm Puteaux SA 1918, as was used with the Renault FT.

The Warsaw-based Instytut Zarządzania Podażą ('Armoured Supply Management') and Biura Badań Technicznych Broni Pancernych ('Armoured Forces Technical Research Offices'), the latter under Captain Rudolf Gundlach, respectively orchestrated the purchasing and oversight of several companies to produce specialized domestic tank components. Much as bell manufacturers once had the transitive experience and equipment to make cannon, locomotive producers and steel foundries were similarly tasked to produce AFVs. Ostrowiec Works and Zieleniewski & Fitzner-Gamper Boilers and Mechanical Works SA contributed blast furnaces, steelworks, iron and steel foundries, locomotive wheels and axles, and iron structures, while Southern Works, Huta SA, Bathory, Pokoj and Baildon made steel. Within Warsaw others provided additional services and goods, including: the Polish Mechanical Association of America (armament); 'Tudor' Battery Works SA; Lilpop Rau & Loewenstein (cast track links); Gerlach Precision Instrument Factory (instrumentation); National Optics Works (wz.37 CA gunsight); and National Tele- and Radio-technical Works 'Ava' (N2/C tank radio sets).

The Wojskowy Nadzór Techniczny ('Military Technical Supervision Department') orchestrated component delivery to PZInż in the Warsaw suburb of Czechowicach, and determined technical specification compliance. Tasked with assembling the 7TP (factory F-1), surrounding plants provided related functions, including F-3 (engines and fittings), F-4 (Factory Truck Ursus) (iron foundry and non-ferrous metals) and F-6 (diesel-engine repair and renovation). In addition to the 7TP, Ursus produced C7P tractors, TKS tankettes, C2P crawler tractors and related vehicle components. Respectively designated PZInż 220 and PZInż 120 for the single- and dual-turret versions, the two 7TP versions were more commonly known as 7TP jw (*jednowieżowy*) and 7TP dw (*dwuwieżowy*).

Although the 7TP design showed promise when compared with contemporary tanks, modern anti-tank guns such as the German 3.7cm PaK 36 and Italian 20mm Breda Modello 35 had proven very effective during the Spanish Civil War (1936–39) and gave senior commanders pause. In spite of the Inspector of the Army, Major-General Tadeusz Piskor, favouring the tank programme's implementation, the head of the Polish Army's General Staff, Brigadier-General Wacław Stachiewicz, lobbied against it, believing the increasing power of anti-tank guns made producing vulnerable, expensive tanks rather pointless. With the project to move cautiously forwards, officials agreed that the 7TP should incorporate a 37mm main gun in a single turret once the latter became available, with funding providing for outfitting just one armoured company. A second series (3/36-37/37/Panc) on 7 February 1936 called for a further 16 dual-turret vehicles (serial numbers 1705–1720) to be delivered by 5 January 1937. Three days later, KSUS (Komitet do Spraw Uzbrojenia i Sprzętu, or 'Committee for Weapons and Equipment') established a detailed programme to develop AFVs, as part of the 1936/37 and 1939/40 budgets; if approved, this would provide for eight battalions totalling 392 7TPs, with 20 more in reserve. With single-turret tank production soon commencing, 14 vehicles from Series 2 were retooled to accept them instead. Subsequent 7TPs would be constructed as single-turret tanks; like the PzKpfw II, the 7TP was to have an offset turret.

With Poland having sold several Renault FTs to Uruguay – although through Soviet buyers who redirected them to Republican forces fighting in Spain – and China during October 1936 and January 1937, Dowództwo Broni Pancernych received

A dual-turret 7TP, pictured during the operation to seize Zaolzie Province for Poland during October 1938. The two white lines on the hull side denote 3rd Armoured Battalion, while the flowers near the opened driver's hatch are an indication of the support offered the Polish forces by the area's predominantly Polish population. (Public Domain)

unexpected funding that provided for the construction for what would be an additional 60 7TPs. During 1937, 67 vehicles were ordered – 18 in Series 3 (1721–1738), and 49 for Series 4 (1739–1787) – with 14 single-turret and two dual-turret tanks produced that year; enough for a second light-tank company by year's end. In June 1938, a final Series 5 ordered 16 vehicles (1788–1803), which provided enough 7TPs to allow the removal of ageing Vickers vehicles from the roster. Although several additional 7TPs were ordered as part of the final production series in April (32), June (100) and August 1939 (50), delays dogged overall production and delivery until the commencement of hostilities in late summer 1939, by which time four prototypes, 108 single-turret and 24 dual-turret tanks had been produced.

Having abandoned what was considered an ineffective Vickers machine-gun armament, between 1933 and 1936 a 13.2mm Hotchkiss variety was tested in 16 dual-turret tanks, with the remaining six each having one turret

Mirroring the PzKpfw II's interior, the 7TP featured a forward compartment for the driver/mechanic; this was located between the transmission, which was accessible via two access panels, and the covered driveshaft. Instead of a separate vision port and access hatch, the vehicle combined the two. (Keystone-France/Gamma-Keystone via Getty Images)

mounting a French wz.18 37mm gun. Following the purchase of 22 British-made turrets, consideration was made to mount various guns, including a 40mm (Vickers or Starachowice Works), 47mm wz.25 'Pocisk' (Bullet), and a 55mm (Starachowice Works), with the Swedish Bofors 37mm eventually chosen. In December 1935, the Swedes were tasked with developing a version suitable for turret mounting, which was sent to Poland in November 1936. It was installed in 'Dragon' in January 1937 and firing tests were successfully conducted between 3 and 17 February. It was deemed suitable for the 7TP and 300 were purchased, while the Polish Mechanical Association of America in Pruszków produced a licensed copy as the wz.37, a variant of the towed wz.36 anti-tank gun. To accommodate the new weapon, the turret was commensurately lengthened as a counterweight, with the space then used to house radios in command vehicles. It also meant replacing the rear hatch with one in the roof. In March 1937 the initial batch of 50 guns was ordered (3001–3050), which the National Armaments Studios' Rifle Factory in Warsaw delivered by 31 March 1938, with 61 more (3051–3111) arriving 12 months after that. A third contract for 75 guns (3112–3186) in April 1939 never materialized, as on 5 September German advances prompted the factory's evacuation.

Having produced an accepted prototype gunsight based on the TWZ-1 Zeiss variety on 10 January 1937, National Optics Works produced 110 wz.37 CA periscope gunsights from 1 October 1938 until the start of hostilities. To improve visibility for the commander/gunner, Captain Rudolf Gundlach produced 400 periscopes for the turret hatch; his design allowed for external rotation through 360 degrees, while the interior viewing mechanism remained stationary. Although the commander/gunner's observation to the outside was poor to the sides and rear, his view was superior to the driver/mechanic's.

TECHNICAL
SPECIFICATIONS

ARMOUR

During a tank's prototype stage, many nations incorporated common boilerplate as a readily available, cheaper substitute for steel to replicate the vehicle's weight for testing various components, and determine optimal configurations. With this level of protection understandably unsuited for use in combat, to provide proper protection against bullets and shrapnel its production hull and turret comprised alloyed steel that included elements such as carbon, chromium and nickel to impart corrosion resistance, strength and durability. For thin armoured plate, this proved effective in resisting high-velocity impacts, as it made for a hard, yet sufficiently flexible, product. Although MAN experimented with sloped armour to improve its equivalent thickness – something the Soviets furthered after Kama's closing for the A-20, and eventually the T-34/76 – early Panzer designs maintained flatter, more easily produced plate. The Poles also incorporated sloped armour; much as with other countries, this was often done on pre-1939 light tanks to test the concept. Based on the experiences in the Spanish Civil War, such thin armour lacked the necessary thickness and strength to resist existing anti-tank rounds, let alone those expected in the near future. As such, a PzKpfw II's battlefield survivability depended on being able to move quickly from one position to another, and make use of terrain to mask its presence, and promote surprise. The heavier and better-armoured PzKpfw III and PzKpfw IV were intended to conduct direct combat operations, although even they proved vulnerable, as the fighting in Poland showed.

PzKpfw II

The PzKpfw II incorporated rolled homogeneous armour (RHA), in which a steel ingot was rolled to a specific thickness along a single direction; this process forced the material's microscopic grains to line up to increase strength, and spread an impact's shock. As a final stage, the plate was subjected to a heat-quenching process that removed imperfections to toughen the metal further. With a Brinell Hardness Number (BHN) of between 340 and 380, the result was something harder than stainless steel, but not to the point of being overly brittle, and susceptible to cracking. Electric welding was used to join the plates together at Daimler-Benz AG.

Various aspects of PzKpfw II testing were undertaken at the Grafenwöhr Training Area, just south of the MAN factory. On impact, sharp-nosed 37mm projectiles overmatched the PzKpfw II's thin armour, and would usually penetrate it outright. Because of their smaller size and mass, non-armour-piercing rifle and machine-gun bullets, while seldom penetrating, could cause spalling, in which steel fragments from a section roughly equivalent to the round's impact area were sprayed inwards. As the PzKpfw II was intended to be an improvement over the PzKpfw I, and was not built for direct action against enemy tanks, all of its armour was essentially ineffective against anything greater than small arms and shrapnel, with the area under the turret front particularly vulnerable. Considering the frontal arc of any tank received the majority of direct-fire anti-tank rounds, additional plate would be added to the hull and turret front of some 70 per cent of PzKpfw II Ausf C tanks in service following the Polish campaign. Even though the PzKpfw II was employed as a stop-gap tank, its possession of a radio receiver and transmitter would allow it to be used within existing German armoured doctrine.

This burned-out PzKpfw II is depicted in Warsaw. The PzKpfw II had armour roughly equivalent to that of other countries' light tanks of the era; France's Renault R 35 possessed thicker plates, but these were still RHA. First installed in the Ausf a/2 prototype, the PzKpfw II's engine compartment acted as a firewall, while deck grating provided additional air circulation for the covered radiator fan. In line with the transmission and driveshaft, the rear-mounted engine was offset to starboard. [Hugo Jaeger/Timepix/The LIFE Picture Collection/Getty Images]

7TP

Instead of RHA, the 7TP incorporated armour made from face-hardened steel alloy infused with chromium, to increase toughness, and nickel, to increase resistance to corrosion and oxidation. This involved a similar rolling process to RHA, after which heating and cooling were applied to the external face, imparting a hard front to promote projectile shattering, while maintaining a softer inner section possessing the flexibility to help absorb impacts. As armour plate was installed based on an anticipated attack angle with a particular calibre of projectile, face hardening resulted in a BHN score of between 360 and 400; such armour was only marginally superior to RHA, and then only at impact angles greater than about 30 degrees. RHA was more prone to spalling, as non-penetrating rounds had a greater chance of deforming the immediate impact area, and this was correspondingly reflected on the interior side.

As former German industry in Upper Silesia possessed decades of experience in mining and metallurgy, Friedenshütte AG, Baildon-Silesia Stahl AG, Bismarck Hütte AG and others were redesignated with Polish names after 1919. These firms would produce the steel armour plate for Poland's AFVs, including the 7TP. The Keller blast furnaces used by some of these manufacturers was key in melting ferromanganese, which as part of their steel-making process improved workability, imparted strength and acted as an imperfection-reducing deoxidizer, making the armour metallurgically similar to that of the PzKpfw II. As Polish industry lacked the equipment and expertise to weld the armour plates during assembly, rivets were used, which resulted in a comparatively weaker bond. While use of rivets was common for the period, projectile impacts unduly stressed these weakened areas, and they could shatter and spray the crew with fragments.

ARMAMENT

The PzKpfw II's 2cm cannon was suited for reconnaissance, and similar peripheral duties, in which it was most likely to encounter soft or static defensive targets, and could deliver a high volume of fire. As with most AFVs a secondary machine gun was included for use against infantry and similar targets. Intended to engage enemy armour directly, the 7TP's 37mm gun – although slower to fire than that of its opponent – provided greater range that made it difficult for the PzKpfw II to close to an effective engagement range, especially over open terrain.

PzKpfw II

Originally created for use in armoured cars, Rheinmetall-Borsig AG's automatic, recoil-operated 2cm KwK 30 L/55 was a shorter-barrelled version of the 2cm Flak 30, an anti-aircraft weapon covertly developed at Waffenfabrik Solothurn AG (Solothurn, Switzerland) during the late 1920s. The PzKpfw II's small turret provided a suitable platform to house the weapon, which rested atop a large support mount, with a cylinder-enclosed recoil spring and brake shoe underneath. To maintain alignment between the KwK 30 and its sight during movement a *Zurrbrücke* (cradle lock frame) connected the gun to the turret roof, where the *Zurrbrücke* could be swung up and

PzKpfw II AMMUNITION

As the most powerful armour-piercing 2cm round available to the Germans, the Swiss Solothurn 20×138mm PzGr 39 138B (**1**), a belted round, produced a chamber pressure of roughly 3,000atm – the equivalent of 44,000psi – with 46.5kJ muzzle energy. Travelling at 780m/sec, it offered a penetrative capability of 20mm@100m, 14mm@500m and 8mm@1,000m. 204mm tall, it had a ZZ 1505 fuse, and was painted black, with a yellow band to indicate it contained an explosive element. Its markings – here reading 'Rh.1c38.148g' – indicated the manufacturer's code, the

shipment code number, the production year and the projectile weight, plus 'Ph' (phosphorus). The Sprgr 39 high-explosive round (**2**) was painted yellow, with a red band. It had an unpainted AZ 5045 nose-detonating steel fuse and 35.9kJ muzzle energy. The labelling – here reading 'Rh.S.1a39.115g' – indicated. Both projectiles used the same-sized brass cartridge, with a percussion cap for triggering. The powder was housed in a two-section fabric bag, with a smaller and larger compartment respectively containing an igniter and main propellant charge.

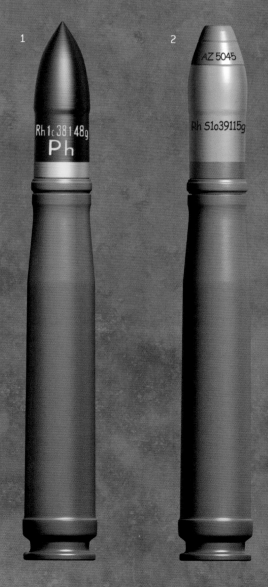

7TP AMMUNITION

The 7TP's main gun produced around 259kJ muzzle energy (compared to the PzKpfw II's 46.5kJ), and a chamber pressure of 2,600atm – the equivalent of 38,000psi. 320mm tall, the 37×257mmR projectile (**1**) was 56mm wide at its base. The 37mm armour-piercing high-explosive round weighed 0.7kg, including a 15g warhead. With a velocity of 800m/sec, it offered a penetrative capability of 60mm@300m, 48mm@500m, 30mm@1,000m and 20mm@2,000m. The armour-piercing tracer round (**2**) had the same basic identification nomenclature – in this case, 'F.A. 1-36'. The high-explosive fragmentation round (**3**) contained a 48g explosive charge that was detonated on impact. It was 350mm tall, and could be fired out to some 7,100m.

SdKfz 232 armoured cars are pictured during a parade past Hitler and other Nazi leaders, including Luftwaffe chief Reichsmarschall Hermann Göring (second row, right). These armoured cars mounted the same 2cm KwK L/55 cannon as the PzKpfw II, and served as part of a *Panzer-Division's Aufklärungs-Abteilung (mot.)* (motorized reconnaissance battalion). (© Michael Nicholson/Corbis)

out of the way when not in use. A box-feed magazine shelf was to port and angled slightly forwards to provide easier access.

The main gun's elevation mechanism provided +20 to -9 degrees, and was similar to that found in small turrets of the period, although rather over-engineered and costly. It comprised a cylinder-enclosed threaded rod that connected the ceiling and gun-support mount. By turning a low-mounted hand wheel a follower surrounding the rod acted on an attached gearbox to help raise or lower the gun, which could be locked in place prior to firing. The wheel-controlled elevation mechanism allowed the main gun (and machine gun) to remain fixed on a target during firing, and helped reduce stress on the turret and mantlet. A traverse hand wheel provided four degrees of rotation per turn. The clutch-activated, manual traverse mechanism could be set to EIN (traverse gear engaged; traverse lock disengaged) and EST (traverse gear disengaged; traverse lock engaged), with AUS (traverse gear disengaged; traverse lock disengaged) allowing for two turret ring handles to provide manual rotation on its ball bearings. The turret could be fully rotated in roughly 40 seconds.

The PzKpfw II carried around 180 Pzgr 39 (*Panzergranate*, armour-piercing) and Sprgr 39 (*Sprenggranate*, high-explosive) rounds. The Pzgr 39 was believed to be able to penetrate contemporary AFVs at common engagement ranges. Although most nations had abandoned anti-tank armour-piercing high-explosive rounds by the mid-1930s, due to their inferior armour penetrative capability compared to solid-shot rounds – and a tendency to shatter on contact – their use with light automatic cannon against aircraft and anti-tank guns remained valid in 1939. As the Flak 30's 20-round magazine was too large for effective use inside the PzKpfw II's small fighting compartment, a ten-round version was used instead; 18 magazines were generally stored along the superstructure and hull in bins and brackets, with each magazine typically all of one type.

Like the 2cm KwK 30 L/55, the 7.92mm MG 34 was produced in great numbers. As the PzKpfw II was designed as an interim tank, incorporating such common weapons systems was logical. Unlike the 7TP's water-cooled secondary machine gun, the air-cooled MG 34 required less effort to operate and maintain. The MG 34 could be removed by the crew to supplement their small arms after abandoning their mount. Belts of MG 34 ammunition were stored in metal drums or 17 150-round canvas ammunition bags; these fed the weapon via a left-side slide receiver. Another (empty) bag was attached to the gun's right to catch spent cartridges and prevent clutter.

7TP

Like the German 3.7cm PaK 36, the Bofors cannon as a towed anti-tank weapon was light and offered a high rate of fire. The 37mm Bofors wz.37 L/45 monobloc cannon comprised a spring-loaded, semi-automatic locking wedge breech that could fire roughly ten rounds per minute. Its sliding block and opening, ejecting case and firing pin, however, were automatic. It was 1,736mm long; its use of a muzzle brake dampened recoil by 16 per cent.

To completely rotate the turret, a knob at the bottom of the worm conveyor drive mechanism needed to be turned seven times, with the aid of a five-gear reducer that redirected some of the motor's energy. A second knob alongside the main armament used a four-gear reducer to provide elevation and depression, with only one rotation required to transition through +25 to -10 degrees. To prevent damage to the complex

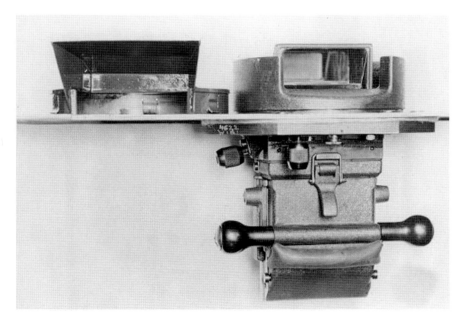

A Gundlach periscope of the variety installed in the 7TP's front turret hatch. The left-hand external hood helped minimize glare and debris on the objective mirror. The interior piece with handles in its upright, space-saving position was flipped down during use. While this section remained stationary, the exterior portion could be rotated 360 degrees. (Public Domain)

PzKpfw II GUNSIGHT

Targeting the KwK 30 main armament was achieved via a centre-mounted, articulated TZF 4/38 gunsight that was bracketed to the turret ceiling to provide the commander/gunner with a consistent viewing position. To compensate for the main gun's vertical movement, the 559mm-long 9kg monocular tube incorporated a flexible elbow and prism, and provided 2.5× magnification, a 25-degree field of view, and a range scale out to '12' (1,200m). The Leitz-produced design was used to target both the cannon and the coaxial machine gun, and included a padded eyepiece for viewing through the right eye, and a black felt cover for the left to minimize eye fatigue from keeping one closed. It also included a forehead pad for the gunner so he could more comfortably maintain visual contact with the target. Hinged mantlet flaps allowed for both the main armament and the coaxial machine gun to be fired over open sights. The KwK 30 was fired via a trigger on the elevating hand wheel, and the MG 34 by a trigger on the traversing wheel on the right.

7TP GUNSIGHT

As the commander pulled double-duty as gunner, he used the vehicle's wz.37 CA gunsight that provided 1.4× magnification and a 30-degree field of view. To accommodate for a moving target a 'Direction of Movement' scale was provided atop the reticle's crosshairs. The commander used the hash marks numbered 0 to 50 (left and right of centre) to adjust and improve the accuracy of rounds against a moving target depending whether it was moving towards or away. While this was only employed when the vehicle was stationary due to the lack of a main-armament stabilizer, the Gundlach periscope atop the turret provided the commander with a 360-degree view, without turning his head, since the internal section remained stationary. The wz.37 gun was aimed by a crank gear, and like the machine gun, fired by a pedal.

system of gears during firing, a sliding gear lever worked with a disc brake to reduce inertia. As hard stops, or similar jarring movements, risked damaging the turret's gear teeth, friction plates were also installed to help minimize such forces. Of the 7TP's 80 rounds, only four were stored in the turret for immediate use. Owing to the radio's placement in the rear extension, the remainder were stored along the fighting compartment's hull in 66 starboard slots.

The 7TP's recoil-operated Ckm (*ciężki karabin maszynowy*, or 'heavy machine gun') wz.30 was an unlicensed copy of the Colt-Browning M1917A1. Modified to fire 7.92×57mm Mauser ammunition from a non-disintegrating fabric belt, it could penetrate 8mm of armour at 200m. Possessing a limited number of parts, a 450rd/min rate of fire and a velocity of 845m/sec, the weapon proved to be an excellent, reliable system, although its 1.2m length and 21kg weight made it awkward to operate optimally within a confined turret. Its barrel had a conical flash suppressor, and it was fired via a pedal. Produced between 1931 and 1939, the wz.30 was mounted into the turret where its armoured, water-cooled radiator, with a 4-litre capacity, projected forward of the mantlet. Although the wz.30 could be removed from the dual-turret version of the 7TP for when having to fight dismounted, it could not be removed by the crews of single-turret 7TPs. The weapon's 330-cartridge fabric belt lacked metal connectors, and retained its integrity after firing. The ammunition was stored in metal boxes against the fighting compartment's hull.

MOBILITY

Considering the thin armour on both the PzKpfw II and 7TP, it was not prudent to engage targets from one location for too long. While the defender had an advantage in that he could fire from a concealed or protected position, with a stable platform, once detected he was at risk of being outmanoeuvred. While the 7TP's longer-ranged main gun could engage the PzKpfw II at distances beyond which the latter could effectively respond, the use of radios and co-ordination with integrated engineer, artillery and reconnaissance elements, as well as tactical air support, meant the Germans would eventually subdue or bypass resistance, which would be made untenable via their more rapid battlefield tempo.

PzKpfw II

The Germans predominantly used petrol engines in tanks, trucks and the like, as these were often derivatives of aircraft designs, which tended to produce greater torque than equivalent diesel motors. The Maybach HL (*Hochleistungsmotor*, or 'overhead line motor') 62 TR (*Trockensumpfschmierung*, or 'dry sump lubrication') 6,191cc petrol engine produced 103kW (sustained)@2,600rpm (11.57kW/tonne). Instead of a wet sump lubrication arrangement, German engineers incorporated a more expensive – and better-performing – 'dry' variety that used an additional reservoir to circulate oil. Its six cylinders imparted a rather limited 6.5:1 compression ratio, which translated into increased fuel consumption, while ignition was via a magneto 12V electric generator. The ZF Aphon SSG 46 manual transmission comprised one reverse and six forward gears, although only second to sixth worked with a synchromesh system in which gears matched each other's rotation speed to provide smoother shifting and less wear for larger vehicles.

Steering relied on an epicyclic, two-plate dry clutch where an actuator forced a pressure plate into a corresponding friction one that connected to the driveshaft and brake. Rising from near the floor-mounted transmission, the tiller/shift lever angled forwards before terminating in a handle that was adjacent to the driver's right grab handle; the mate being to his left. Pulling back on one engaged the epicyclical clutch to slow that side's drive sprocket, or apply the respective brake if additional force was used, and cause a turn of varying sharpness. Near each pivot, a curved toothed component kept the lever in the desired position during turning. An accelerator, clutch and brake were located on the floor, which had a raised, slip-resistant diamond pattern. The main instrument panel had a large speedometer for improved visibility in what was a dim, smoky compartment during action, with a starter to the driver's right against the transmission. In addition to opening the vision slit, having the hull access hatch open provided additional visibility when driving. To the driver's right, a knob-topped gearshift and disengaging grip lever was set into the transmission's side.

The PzKpfw II Ausf C had quarter-elliptic leaf-spring suspension (essentially half of a symmetrical curved variety). Composed of stacked steel strips of increasing lengths, with a roller holding the longest in place, it provided a simple solution, in which a single bell crank housed the opposite end with all the leafs terminated. Here, a wheel set behind a pivot provided independent vertical movement, and above each axle a hull-anchored catch kept the apparatus from extending too far when travelling

Owing to the unusually hot and sunny summer of 1939, the region's low water levels meant that many rivers that were usually unfordable could now be negotiated. The PzKpfw II could operate in nearly a metre of water. A PzKpfw I Ausf A (foreground) and PzKpfw II (likely from PzRgt 36, 4. Panzer-Division) cross the Bzura River on 10 September 1939. During the battle, the formation operated alongside Infanterie-Regiment (mot.) *Leibstandarte-SS Adolf Hitler.* (Library of Congress)

over rough terrain. While able to hold considerable weight, exposure to the elements meant the leaves were prone to rusting; this inhibited their ability to slide against each other and properly absorb movement, while also making them vulnerable to combat damage. Each track comprised 105 dry-pin (non-lubricated) track links, with 2,400×300mm of ground contact.

7TP

One necessary improvement over the original Vickers design was the inclusion of a new longitudinally mounted, liquid-cooled, six-cylinder, four-stroke diesel engine. Factory-designated the PZInż. 235, the Saurer VBLDb 8,550cc motor incorporated fuel injection, and provided 81kW@1,800rpm (8.28kW/tonne). The resulting power was transmitted from the engine to a four-speed gearbox at the driver's position via a shielded steel driveshaft. For optimal operation, each gear had a maximum recommended vehicle speed: first, 7km/h; second, 13km/h; third, 22km/h; and fourth, 37km/h. A 170-litre fuel tank was along the hull's starboard side near the driver's seat, with two fuel filler necks rising up to the superstructure deck. A 20-litre fuel reserve buttressed against the gearbox, which combined for some 22 litres of fuel for each hour of engine operation.

The 7TP's engine provided an additional 20hp (15kW) than an equivalent petrol variety, and its fuel was less flammable, but the decision to use it was based on the limited availability of domestically produced petrol motors. During the 1930s no accommodation was provided for producing diesel engines for heavy vehicles, as it would present a considerable logistic problem by having to provide both duel types. The Polish General Staff had also created studies that stressed domestic industry lacked the necessary manufacturing sophistication and capabilities to produce diesel engines, even though they would be better suited to heavier tanks and tractors.

Steering was done via alternating clutch and brake using a lever to the driver's left and right, which imparted a maximum 2.5m turning radius. The gearshift was just ahead of

the latter, while on the floor a pedal connected into the forward drive axle. The fuel pump and main clutch control rods extended from near the driver's feet to the main clutch adjacent to the engine. A starter button was located to port of the two-piece driver's hatch, with the upper door having a sight for when buttoned up. When it was open, the driver could sit forward to gain better visibility when operating outside of a combat zone.

The 7TP's suspension comprised two primary cast rocker arms, each with two bogies and a pair of rubber-rimmed road wheels. Connecting the locomotive-style bogies, a half-leaf suspension provided simple, reliable support, although its complex design made maintenance difficult. The vehicle had a forward drive sprocket, a rear idler and four rubber wheel return rollers. Modelled on those used by its Vickers precursor, each of the 7TP's tracks comprised centralized alignment teeth and 109 links, with 2,900×267mm of ground contact.

Dual-turret Vickers Mark E tanks on the move during a pre-war exercise. A fuel pump and electric generator were housed alongside the motor, behind which a large, vertical water-cooled radiator bisected the compartment where a hose ran aft to the cooling fan guard and drive. On the engine deck, a protective external mesh helped keep larger debris from entering the cooling system, just forward of the muffler. (Three Lions/Getty Images)

THE COMBATANTS

TRAINING AND ETHOS

GERMAN

The first *Kraftfahrkampftruppenschule* (Motorized Combat Troop School) was established in October 1936 at Wünsdorf, near Berlin, which trained all ranks as tankers, anti-tank gunners, motorized personnel and motorcycle personnel. The facility supervised the recently established Schießlehrgang (Gunnery Instruction Course) Putlos on the North Sea. In 1937, the school split into Panzertruppenschule Wünsdorf – covering armour training and doctrine, and motorization issues – and Kavallerieschule Döberitz (jointly 'owned' by the *Panzertruppe* and the Cavalry) for cavalry, motorized infantry and motorized reconnaissance issues. In 1938 the latter facility was moved a few kilometres south to Krampnitz.

As part of Germany's Wehrkreis (military district) system, *Panzerwaffe* recruitment was conducted geographically, with volunteers or conscripts generally ending up in the local unit. These comprised *Berufssoldaten* (career soldiers) and *Auf Kriegsdauer* (for the conflict's duration). The initial personnel were drawn from cavalry regiments that had been mechanized to become *Panzer-Regimenter*. Following call-up all Heer recruits went through common basic training that was conducted by their division's *Ersatz-Abteilung* (replacement battalion); this stressed discipline, weapons use, small unit tactics and practical training. As recruits tended to enter basic training already fit, sports was emphasized and physical conditioning pushed them to their limits. Basic training involved drill, firearms and live-fire exercises, and – unlike most other armies of the period – the Heer encouraged individual initiative, leadership and an eagerness for responsibility. To reinforce independent thought, instructors placed recruits in

unfamiliar or disorienting situations and evaluated their performance. Training was seriously impaired, however, by the scarcity of NCOs and the fact that many officers were transferred to the Luftwaffe, and many older former officers who returned to active duty proved to be unsuited for permanent service.

After basic training the recruit went to his parent unit and began six months of intense infantry training, including operating the 3.7cm anti-tank gun. Emphasis was placed on operating within combined-arms *Kampfgruppen* (battlegroups) at various organizational levels – including armour, combat-engineer and anti-tank assets – to ensure the various parties understood the function and capabilities of the other unit types. All personnel in the *Ersatz-Abteilung* received extensive infantry instruction to ensure everyone could fight if necessary, thereby also providing potential combat replacements for the arm of service likely to suffer the greatest number of casualties – the infantry. On its completion, the men were broken into groups, where some 45 per cent received specialist anti-tank training, 40 per cent went on to become vehicle drivers and mechanics, and the remainder became signalmen. Initial driver training was on PzKpfw I and II that had their turret and superstructure removed, with additional instruction on tank maintenance. Panzer training was very structured, initially individually, and then as part of a crew, with unit-level exercises and large manoeuvres following. In 1937 the first large-scale tank training manoeuvres were held around Neustrelitz. Individual tank commanders were chosen from among the best-trained tank crewmen, with the *Zugführer* (platoon leader) selected from the best commanders.

POLISH

In the early 1930s CWBrPanc at Modlin was established under Lieutenant-Colonel (qual.) ('qualified', indicating a War College graduate) Jerzy Levittoux, Lieutenant-Colonel (qual.) Karol Hodala and Lieutenant-Colonel (qual.) Antoni Korczyński. Initially, an experimental battalion was formed for training, which fielded Vickers

Several post-1939 PzKpfw II crossing a ditch, with the two nearest being Ausf C tanks. Owing to the dusty conditions cloth has been wrapped around each barrel's end to prevent fouling. The nearest vehicle carries a spare road wheel. The *Kraftfahrkampftruppenschule* at Krampnitz offered four courses, including a tactical introductory phase that provided officers from other Heer branches with insight into armour capabilities, and a training phase for Panzer officers to receive theoretical and practical instruction. A technical course provided younger NCOs that had passed an entrance examination, theory and practice in caring for vehicles, while the NCOs of all motorized units were trained as master mechanics. In addition, enlisted personnel that had passed initial driver tests were admitted for motor-transport instruction and experimentation. A final course focused on tank firing instruction. (Nik Cornish at www.stavka.org.uk)

PzKpfw II TURRET LAYOUT

The commander/gunner and loader/radio operator occupied the central fighting compartment, which had a raised deck to accommodate for a sub-floor. The turret was offset to port due to the driveshaft tunnel extending along the floor between the transmission and engine. Unlike some other designs, the PzKpfw II had no turret basket separating it from the hull to make rotation less taxing on the crew and better contain the fighting compartment. The commander/gunner sat in a height-adjustable padded seat suspended by rear-mounted tubes, which originally had a seatbelt restraint to be used when moving over rough terrain. Turret access was through a double rectangular roof hatch, with one incorporating a flare pistol flap, and rounds stored in a box along the turret rear. A simple rotating periscope sat just ahead, and although it provided adequate forward visibility, the turret restricted view to the sides.

Doubling as the main gun's loader, the loader/radio operator sat directly behind and away from the driver/mechanic, and had a vision flap overlooking the vehicle's rear. A Morse-code key pad was located above the radio storage cabinet near a bracket-mounted fire extinguisher. The commander/gunner's headphones and throat microphones were stored in a box near his seat's support bracket, while to its right was an electrical junction and connect boxes for radio equipment. Turret insignia is omitted here for clarity.

1. Bevelled vision flap
2. Turret-removal hooks
3. Turret hatch
4. 2cm KwK 30 L/55
5. Main-gun cradle
6. Mantlet
7. Direct-vision flap handle
8. Muzzle-flash suppressor
9. Turret-ring traverse teeth
10. TZF 4/38 sight
11. 7.92mm MG 34 (coaxial)
12. MG 34 gurtsack (ammunition bags)
13. Flat flap
14. Traverse mechanism
15. Traverse hand wheel
16. Commander's headset and throat microphone storage box
17. Commander's seat

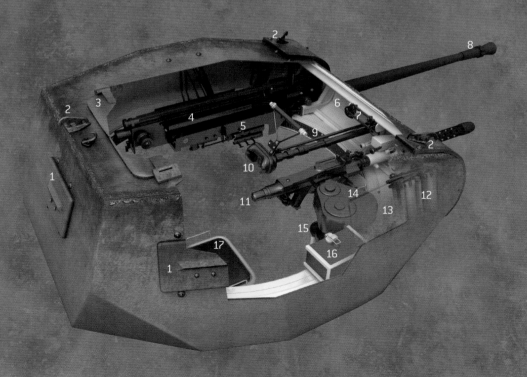

7TP TURRET LAYOUT

The commander/gunner was to the turret's starboard, alongside the loader, with the commander/gunner using a rotating Gundlach periscope, and the loader a fixed episcope. Although only two crewmen occupied the position, much of the coaxial machine gun and the main gun's breech protruded into the fighting compartment, making for a confined working environment. To offer a degree of protection for the loader during firing, a horizontal plate offered separation from the sliding breech block, which accepted shells and ejected spent casings via a lever. To keep the latter from further cluttering the turret, they were sent along a tubular device to a waiting collection basket.

1. Loader's seat
2. Turret locking pedal
3. 37mm spent-cartridge container
4. Traverse wheel/turret drive mechanism
5. 37mm Bofors wz.37 L/45 cannon
6. Armoured 7.92mm Ckm wz.30 MG radiator
7. 7.92mm Ckm wz.30 MG
8. Wz.37 CA gunsight
9. Protective breech recoil plate
10. Spent MG cartridge container
11. Spent 37mm wz.37 cartridge chute
12. Loader's episcope
13. Armoured ventilation housing
14. Jib crane socket
15. Gundlach periscope
16. Turret hatch (non-personnel)
17. 15mm armoured turret band

7TPs of 3rd Armoured Battalion on exercises in the Błędów Desert, north-west of Kraków, in 1939. The Germans subsequently used the terrain, similar to that of North Africa, for training elements of the Deutsches Afrikakorps elements prior to their service in Libya. (Public Domain)

reconnaissance TK tankette companies and a company of wz.29 armoured cars. Under Major Antoni Śliwiński, and later Major Stefan Majewski III, the unit operated as 11th Armoured Battalion. In August 1935, the facility received its first 7TP prototype, 'Elephant'. Once the initial four 7TP series-production runs were completed, the vehicles were sent to 3rd Armoured Battalion in Warsaw in September 1935. Four dual-turret 7TPs from the first series were added to 11th Armoured Battalion, with cadets 'on loan' from 3rd Armoured Battalion.

After a training programme conducted between 30 August 1936 and 30 June 1939, the cadets emerged as well-trained infantry. Additional instruction was conducted at the Biedrusk armoured camp near Poznań, which focused almost exclusively on motorized coursework, and practical experience operating their mounts in combat simulations in a variety of environments and terrain. Initially, Vickers tanks were used, but as more 7TPs became available they steadily supplanted the ageing British vehicles. Here, the tankers practised targeting and firing their 37mm main gun, including while moving, something impractical for the period unless warranted by special circumstances, and night-time exercises, without the use of lights. In addition to lectures and tactical exercises, map reading and direction finding were stressed, in part due to the command-and-control difficulties posed by fighting at night. Crew training within individual 7TPs, and as part of a platoon, reinforced group bonding, which through repeated drill were intended to make functioning during the chaos of combat second nature.

Exercises were structured to be challenging, with some of the most difficult being performing tank maintenance from inside a 'buttoned-up' vehicle. In addition to the occasional commemoration parade during the late 1930s, sufficient numbers of 7TPs enabled exercises in company- and battalion-sized grouping to be conducted. 3rd Armoured Battalion staged a two-company demonstration with 32 vehicles, which along with other supporting armour totalled 112 tanks and armoured cars.

DOCTRINE AND TACTICS

GERMAN

As a continuation of longstanding battle-of-annihilation principles, German operational doctrine promoted the destruction of enemy forces via an encircling war of movement. As part of this *Kesselschlacht* ('cauldron battle'), flanking attacks and movement were viewed as superior to firepower in achieving the goal. To achieve an initial penetration, a *Schwerpunkt* ('main focus') was chosen as a defined area in which maximum concentration and effort was directed. Specific march orders were organized to ensure an efficient undertaking and economy of force, and as a prerequisite staff officers were required to submit detailed analysis of the situation from which senior commanders specified the mission objectives. As part of such *Auftragstaktik* (mission-oriented tactics), these cascaded down the ranks as each echelon determined the best way to implement its orders, and most effectively adapt to unfolding battlefield situations. How each achieved their specific sub-mission was generally left to their judgement. As no plan remains intact once an action starts, set-piece orders served little purpose on a fluid battlefield.

Although the Schlieffen Plan had bogged down into static trench warfare in 1914, Seeckt refused to believe that defence was superior to offence, or that large contemporary armies would assure battlefield victory. Instead of masses of largely inexperienced personnel lacking the endurance and resources to exploit tactical battlefield successes, Seeckt put his faith in well-trained mobile formations, believing them most likely to set a rapid battlefield tempo that the enemy would be hard pressed to match. Consequently, official German doctrine accorded very little to conducting a defensive fight, and viewed

A PzKpfw II (left) with a subdued *Balkenkreuz* and PzKpfw III Ausf B sporting an early 'dustbin' cupola are pictured ahead of a destroyed bridge span. A DKW NZ 350 motorcycle stands in the foreground. In concert with such armoured elements, these motorcycles provided for reconnaissance, and facilitated communications; especially during offensive operations, as laying phone lines was comparatively too slow to impart sufficient effectiveness. (Christian Ankerstjerne)

SOLDAT WALTER SANDER

ABOVE Soldat Walter Sander wearing the early-war *Schutzmütze*, a black wool beret covering a padded protective helmet. The *Totenkopf* collar pin – reminiscent of the previous war's tank corps, and earlier Hussars (light cavalry) – together with his black, double-breasted *Panzerjacke*, served to distinguish *Panzertruppen* from their comrades in other arms of service. (Public Domain)

During the Polish campaign, Soldat Walter Sander served in PzRgt 2 (1. Panzer-Division); the formation crossed the border on 1 September 1939 near Grunsruh, and crossed a temporary bridge over the Liswarta River to attack Kłobuck, just south of the Mokra Woods. Over the next few days, PzRgt 2 crossed several creeks and rivers to pass Radomsko, and arrive before an important road junction at Piotrków on 5 September. The next day the unit helped encircle the city, which subsequently fell, and within two days had advanced to the Wisła River for a brief rest. With Polish forces withdrawing on their capital city from the west threatened with encirclement along the Bzura River, the regiment was redirected to the north-east where it helped contain and eliminate the threat.

The following month, he returned to Eisenach where his unit underwent training and incorporated replacements, before moving to Westphalia to conduct wargames in preparation for combat in the West. Sander fought at Sedan and Arras in May 1940, before heading south to Paris and Orléans. On 1 October 1940, PzRgt 2 was allocated to 16. Panzer-Division, which participated in *Barbarossa* and remained in combat throughout the winter. Still serving in PzRgt 2, now as an *Obergefreiter*, during the fighting south of Kharkov, Sander was killed on 27 May 1942. On 1 August 1942 he was posthumously awarded the Ostmedaille, otherwise known as the Frozen Meat Award, for service the previous winter.

such eventualities as simply a lull in offensive action, and a time to resupply or reposition for future attacks. This mentality also promoted a near-slavish desire to conduct rapid counter-attacks to retake lost ground before the enemy could consolidate their gains.

In practice, German armour was expected to provide exploitation after having created a breach in enemy defences, or had supporting units provide an initial opening. Once free of a congested main battle zone, the Panzers were to eliminate targets of opportunity – including command-and-control, logistics and reserve elements – to confuse and demoralize the enemy. With a variety of inherent unit types – combat engineer, artillery, reconnaissance, maintenance, medical and anti-tank – that could reorganize as needed, Panzer formations possessed the flexibility to adjust to, and overcome, most battlefield contingencies, while the strengths of one could compensate for the limitations of the other. By co-ordinating with tactical air elements, reconnaissance was greatly expanded, and rapid reaction ground interdiction was possible. To provide guidelines for a *Panzer-Division*'s expected use, a 24 November 1938 memorandum stated that such formations were to be committed in the most important operational sectors to widen and exploit a breakthrough in the enemy front lines.

CAPTAIN ANTONI PRÓCHNIEWICZ

Antoni Próchniewicz (27 July 1898–2 April 1940) was born in the village of Dminini, some 120km east of Warsaw, and graduated from the nearby high school at Łukowa. He served in 2nd Lancer Regiment during the Russo-Polish War. In 1921 and 1922 Próchniewicz underwent training at the Szkoła Podchorążych Piechoty (Unitarian Infantry Cadet School) in Warsaw, and starting on 1 September 1923 attended NCO training at the Centrum Wyszkolenia Kawalerii (Central Cavalry School) at Grudziądz. Upon graduation he was made a second lieutenant on 1 September 1925, and was posted to the 27th Lancer Regiment, stationed in Nieśwież. In 1930–31 he attended CWBrPanc at Modlin, and following graduation was promoted to captain. Just prior to the outbreak of war in September 1939 he assumed command of 1/2nd LTB.

Four days after the commencement of hostilities, 1/2nd LTB finally arrived at the front lines to engage German reconnaissance elements moving on Piotrków from the south-west. Although the 7TP dominated the PzKpfw II, overwhelming German numbers and assets forced the Polish battalion to fall back on Warsaw. Losses due to combat, and inadequate maintenance and fuel supplies, thinned 1/2nd LTB's strength as it withdrew across the Wisła River a few days later. Having fought during the withdrawal through Warsaw, and into eastern Poland, Próchniewicz was captured heading for the Hungarian border, and spent the next six months in NKVD captivity at Kozelsk, Russia. The Soviets executed him, along with some 22,000 fellow soldiers, police and others, at a remote Russian forest near Katyn, in an effort to control eastern Poland and eliminate future threats to Soviet authority. He was awarded the Cross of Merit in Silver for exemplary civic achievement, left behind a wife, Stefania, and a son, George, and was buried at the Polski Cmentarz Wojenny alongside his comrades.

ABOVE During the Polish campaign, Captain Antoni Próchniewicz commanded 1/2nd LTB in its delaying actions against elements of 1. Panzer-Division and 4. Panzer-Division. (Public Domain)

With defensive armoured operations doctrinally designated as the preparation for a counter-attack, only the attack held merit, of which three basic options existed. To rapidly gain – or pre-empt an enemy's effort to attain – an advantage during a meeting engagement, usually of company to battalion strength. An immediate attack, generally without waiting for follow-on support forces to catch up, hinged on combat readiness to transition rapidly from a march, and to achieve concentration of forces at the desired time and location. Such attacks were generally conducted using a *Keil* (wedge), with one Panzer company forward and two on the flanks, or an inverted *Breitkeil* which presented a wider frontage of two Panzer companies in a wedge flanking a company in an inverted wedge. A final attack choice was reserved for tackling prepared defences, in which the armoured battalion was to engage as part of a combined-arms *Kampfgruppen*. In smaller groupings, fire and movement proved an effective tactic, in which one tank or group of AFVs provided alternating stationary fire support for another.

During the Spanish Civil War, German personnel were to train Nationalist crews for using the PzKpfw I, but once instruction was completed the instructors eventually transitioned to combat duties, which provided valuable combat lessons, such as the benefit of incorporating tactical aircraft and artillery to support armoured and motorized operations. Specific to armour, several deficiencies were uncovered; these included inadequate crew training, the need to repair vehicles that lacked the durability for sustained combat operations, and the requirement to provide logistics capable of maintaining an offensive.

Every subordinate PzKpfw II tank had an FuG 2 (*Funkgerät*, 'receiver'), with a 1.4m aerial, and a WT and RT range of 4km and 2km, respectively. Command tanks were also fitted with a FuG 5 comprising an ultra-short-wave receiver, with headphone and speaker cord attachments, and a 10-watt transmitter. The latter was also attached to a 2m antenna and power cords, and the same range as the FuG 2.

POLISH

Having maintained close political and financial ties with the French following World War I – as well as having received considerable training and support from them – Poland's senior commanders unsurprisingly adopted their ally's armoured doctrine and tactics for their British-based 7TPs. Such instruction promoted an operational mentality of static attrition in which, it was believed, an attacker could be progressively fought down and defeated. Polish tank formations, limited as they were, would serve to bolster key sectors of the front, rather than act as a concentrated force to provide a mobile punch when needed. The Russo-Polish War similarly guided subsequent Polish doctrine, as evidenced by some 10 per cent of forces in September 1939 being cavalry. A lack of motorized elements also meant artillery remained overwhelmingly horse-drawn, with a few options such as the C7P.

Owing to the unavailability of vehicle radios until just before hostilities commenced, only theoretical instruction in their inter-vehicle use, and with command elements, had been provided. To supplement the few radios in use during combat, coloured signal flags were employed for visual communication. The Polish Army invested scant money towards signals equipment, which meant most communication was done via runners, signal flags, including those affixed to the turret, or heliograph, with field

Using the same chassis as the 7TP, the C7P artillery tractor was used to tow Škoda 220mm wz.32 heavy mortars or disabled tanks. Although the C7P was relatively inexpensive to produce, a lack of funds meant only 150 were built. Sporting an olive, green and sand camouflage pattern, these two examples are pictured in Warsaw. (Christian Ankerstjerne)

telephones being relegated to more fixed positions. As such, close proximity and line of sight were important for co-ordinating inter-vehicle actions. Command vehicles were sometimes equipped with domestically produced RKBc or newer N2/C varieties, with each having a respective voice and key range of 6km and 25km.

STRUCTURE, MOBILIZATION AND LOGISTICS

GERMAN

By September 1939 three basic *Panzer-Division* organizations had been devised, in part due to a lack of available vehicles and equipment, but also to determine which configuration proved best. Of the five *Panzer-Divisionen* available, three – including 1. Panzer-Division and 4. Panzer-Division – each fielded one *Panzer-Brigade* of two *Panzer-Regimenter*, each with two *Panzer-Abteilungen*. Each division also possessed a *Schützen-Brigade* to add complementary motorized infantry, and an *Artillerie-Regiment* armed with 10.5cm and 15cm field guns. Some possessed a *Kradschützen-Bataillon* (motorcycle battalion) for reconnaissance, and all had integrated anti-tank, combat-engineer, signals and reconnaissance battalions, as well as services and support units.

To provide for as much flexibility and rapid reaction as possible, German formations comprised a mix of unit types down to company level. Due to the preponderance of PzKpfw I and PzKpfw II tanks, a 1939 Panzer battalion comprised two light companies, along with an 'a' (effectively, a medium) company and a *Staffel* (echelon) element that

This PzKpfw IV Ausf B of 1. leichte Division is probably pictured at Głowaczów, after engaging 7TPs on 9 September. OKH regulation H.M. 1939, Nr. 770 officially replaced the white *Balkenkreuz* markings with a black bordered variety. The 7TP's main gun could penetrate the PzKpfw IV's 14.5mm glacis with little effort. (Christian Ankerstjerne)

also included heavier PzKpfw III and PzKpfw IV tanks. Integrated maintenance and supply units provided support to keep the fighting elements in the field.

POLISH

The Polish light-tank battalion's headquarters component included a mix of support personnel, including motorcycle messengers, traffic and communications personnel and anti-aircraft defence, plus an integrated quartermaster component to provide focused logistical support. It fielded three light-tank companies, each with 16 7TPs. Intended to operate independently under higher commands, such units conducted their own training and maintenance on their various armoured and soft-skinned vehicles. Accordingly, a technical-logistics company was also provided, which comprised a technical platoon, and a supply platoon that had two heavy machine guns (HMGs) and provided additional supplies and reserve crews.

Between 24 and 26 August 1939, 3rd Armoured Battalion mobilized as part of Plan 'W' between Ożarów and Okuniew, with a manpower strength of 462 (including 22 officers) and 49 7TP tanks. Subsequently renamed 1st LTB, the unit possessed 56 7TPs – 26 in reserve mobilization and 23 transitioning from Modlin, plus six dual-turret 7TPs and the 'Elephant' prototype. 1st LTB was commanded by Major Adam Kubin; the adjutant/ADC was First Lieutenant (res.) (reserve) Witold Pajewski and the Tactical and Reconnaissance Officer was Captain Kazimierz Rosen-Zawadzki, who took over command after Kubin was wounded on 8 September. The battalion was disbanded on 10 September. Trained staff personnel and tank drivers were in particularly short supply, and many 7TPs and other battalion vehicles required maintenance, or their main guns to be mounted.

On 15 August 1939, 2nd Armoured Battalion possessed 57 7TPs at Żurawica; this included 26 single-turret 7TPs in reserve mobilization, plus 21 single- and two dual-turret examples sent from Modlin, while seven dual-turret tanks remained at the facility. On 27 August, it was redesignated 2nd LTB; like 1st LTB it had a manpower strength of 462 (including 22 officers) and fielded 49 7TPs. A lack of ammunition meant 2nd LTB set out for combat with only one day's allotment of ammunition, and only company and platoon commanders' tanks received radios. The battalion was commanded by Major Edmund Karpow. His adjutant/ADC was Second Lieutenant Ludwik Szeliga-Natanson and his Tactical and Reconnaissance Officer was Captain Mieczysław Słupski. The battalion was disbanded on 11 September.

The remaining 7TPs (eight dual-turrets, two single-turrets and 'Dragon') were allocated to 11th Armoured Battalion at Modlin, and ended up fighting in Warsaw. At the outset of the campaign, Poland's mobilization plans called for the establishment of a mobile defensive force to protect Warsaw. Tasked by the Dowództwo Obrony Warszawy (Command of the Defence of Warsaw) with organizing its 2nd Light Tank Company (2nd LTC), Captain Stanisław Grąbczewski used the 11 single-turret 7TPs that had recently completed trials at Fort Wola, even though many lacked components, including radios. A second formation was similarly created from the seven dual-turret varieties from the Modlin facility. Designated 1st Light Tank Company (1st LTC), it was commanded by Captain of Horse Feliks Michałkowski and allocated as a third-line reserve as part of an improvised armour/motorized battlegroup; 1st LTC and 2nd LTC were partnered with a tankette complement, and 13th Anti-Tank Company.

These Polish TKS light reconnaissance tankettes were captured by the motorized troops of IR 76, a unit of 20. Infanterie-Division (mot.), at the village of Zaręby-Bolędy. On 1 September 1939 Poland fielded 620 tanks, including obsolete Carden-Loyd Mk VI, Vickers E and 6-ton, and Renault FT models, and 440 TK and TKS tankettes. During mobilization, Polish armoured formations struggled with several issues, including frequent changes in armour and equipment configurations, and personnel assignments; an inability to fill staff positions hampered command and control. As a result, many tankers had little experience with their mounts, with visual recognition and familiarity with explosives found to be lacking. (© IWM MH 18246)

THE STRATEGIC SITUATION

In the months following the Armistice of 11 November 1918, Poland and Germany experienced very different fortunes. As part of the Versailles Treaty, Germany was forced both to admit culpability in starting the war and to relinquish territory. While Germany's new Weimar regime struggled to contain a Communist-inspired revolution that had recently swept westwards from Russia, the newly independent Poles took control of Greater Poland, West Prussia, much of Upper Silesia and the port of Danzig/Gdańsk. Although Polish military forces had seen early successes in Belorussia, Galicia, Ukraine and Czechoslovakia, the Russian Bolsheviks turned their attention towards regaining lost territory, and funnelled forces westwards. During the ensuing Russo-Polish War, on 20 January 1920 the Versailles Treaty took effect; this officially established Poland, with a Western-style parliamentary government, and a land corridor to the Baltic Sea that geographically isolated East Prussia from Germany proper. To help ensure Poland's survival, the Franco-Polish Military Alliance of 1921 stipulated mutual assistance should the other country be attacked; a related secret pact focused against the greatest threats to both nations – Germany and the Soviet Union. As further insurance against having to fight a two-front war, on 25 January 1932 Poland signed a non-aggression treaty with the Soviet Union, and two years later with Germany.

Although Germany's reparations payments were formally suspended as an acknowledgement of the international difficulties caused by the Great Depression, newly elected Chancellor Adolf Hitler's 1933 speech to the Reichstag questioned the Versailles Treaty's legality, and stressed it was the cause of Germany's economic woes. Exploiting France's unwillingness to participate in disarmament talks, Germany withdrew from the League of Nations. With the League having occupied Germany's industrialized Saar region for the last 15 years, in early 1935 its inhabitants overwhelmingly voted to remain within the Weimar Republic, in what was the first of several German territorial reacquisitions. In March that year Hitler openly violated the Versailles Treaty by introducing conscription, calling for expanding the Heer to 500,000 soldiers, and announcing the foundation of the Luftwaffe (air force) and Panzerwaffe (armoured force). Although Hitler and his senior commanders had envisaged occupying the Rhineland in 1937, he ordered it in early 1936 in response to the recent ratification of the Franco-Soviet Treaty of Mutual Assistance, which allowed him to present the endeavour as necessary to protect Germany from becoming encircled.

With Germany's *Panzertruppen* having officially existed for just one year, Hitler sought to distract attention from domestic issues and his territorial acquisitions in Central Europe. Soon after civil war erupted in Spain in July 1936, Germany began sending in powerful air and armoured units, as part of the Condor Legion, which contributed greatly to General Franco's early successes. On 7 October, 41 PzKpfw I Ausf A tanks arrived in-theatre, where they were organized into a battalion of two companies, and entered combat at Madrid on 1 November. Although they were effective against poorly equipped infantry, during encounters with the T-26 – the licensed Soviet iteration of the Vickers 6-ton – they made a bad impression, as little more than 'mobile coffins'. Desiring to see the Nationalist cause succeed, but wanting to balance military support against possibly triggering a wider war, Hitler limited his involvement, and instead encouraged Italian dictator Benito Mussolini to offer proxy support. With German participation contributing to Franco's Nationalists achieving victory in early 1939, the Panzer forces gained valuable battlefield experience, especially with tactical air support of ground operations, and the use of armoured formations.

While the Spanish Civil War raged, Hitler continued to integrate former – and new – territory into the growing Reich. By 1938, Germany, and right-wing elements within Austria, pressured that country's government into agreeing to a vote for union, which once passed preceded German ground forces entry into the region on 12 March to an enthusiastic welcome. With Austria integrating with Germany the following year, the Führer threatened to unleash a European war unless the Sudetenland, a heavily fortified mountainous strip of territory bordering Czechoslovakia and containing an oppressed ethnic German majority, was relinquished to Germany. The leaders of Britain, France, Italy and Germany held a conference in Munich on 29–30 September 1938 and agreed to the annexation, in exchange for Hitler's pledge of peace.

While the Germans annexed the Sudetenland, Poland settled its own territorial disputes with Czechoslovakia, invading and taking control of the disputed districts of

Poland's foremost soldier and statesman, Marshal Józef Piłsudski (1867–1935), is pictured with Generalmajor Max Schindler, the German military attache, and others in May 1933, following a conference to discuss military issues. Piłsudski masterminded Poland's victory in the Russo-Polish War and exerted a profound influence over Poland's governance and relationships with other countries right up to his death in May 1935. By 16 August 1920 the Bolsheviks had advanced to Warsaw and were preparing to overrun the capital; Piłsudski suddenly launched a decisive counter-attack, routing the Bolshevik army and culminating in Europe's final cavalry battle, before pushing the Red Army back to near where it had started, forcing the Bolsheviks into signing an armistice on 12 October.
(© Bettmann/CORBIS)

OPPOSITE Officially established on 2 September, Generaloberst Fedor von Bock's Heeresgruppe Nord employed 4. Armee to sever the Polish Corridor from the rest of the country, and 3. Armee to push south and south-east from East Prussia. In concert, from around Breslau and south to the Carpathian Mountains, Generaloberst Gerd von Rundstedt's Heeresgruppe Süd undertook mirrored operations using 8. Armee, 10. Armee and 14. Armee. In September 1939, seven Polish armies, each named for its operating region or prominent city, were fielded, along with numerous other formations, such as regional operational groups and national-defence brigades, stretched along the borders of East Prussia, Germany proper and Slovakia. As the Polish High Command's General Reserve south of Warsaw, Prusy Army rushed to complete its mobilization; Łódź Army was to fight for time by slowing the German advance, while a main defensive line along the Narew, Wisła and San rivers was established. Tasked with conducting a fighting withdrawal to buy time for Britain and France to invade western Germany, Polish forces were to fall back into central Poland where Warsaw's industrial region would serve as a redoubt, while the open spaces to the east provided a final combat zone in which to reorganize and fight on.

Single-turret 7TPs of 3rd Armoured Battalion parading in the recently occupied Czech city of Český Těšín (known as Czeski Cieszyn to the Poles) during the Zaolzie Campaign (8–13 October 1938). (Public Domain)

Těšín/Cieszyn, Orava/Orawa and Spiž/Spisz. On 6 January 1939, Reich Minister for Foreign Affairs, Joachim von Ribbentrop, and his Polish equivalent, Józef Beck, met in Munich. The Germans wanted to see Danzig/Gdańsk returned to Germany, and proposed the construction of an extraterritorial road and rail line to connect Germany to East Prussia; in exchange, Ribbentrop would agree to all of Poland's existing regional economic conditions. Beck refused to agree to either of these concessions.

On 15 March 1939, Hitler declared the Czech provinces of Moravia and Bohemia a German protectorate, and incorporated them in violation of the Munich agreement. Slovakia became an independent state that was closely allied with Germany and Hungary; the latter then annexed territory in southern Slovakia and seized the Transcarpathian Ukraine. With Czechoslovakia effectively having ceased to exist, German forces occupied the Memel Territory in Lithuania, in what was Hitler's final non-war acquisition. With German territory nearly back to its 1870 borders, the Führer raised territorial demands against Poland, including annexing Danzig/Gdańsk and physically reconnecting Germany proper with East Prussia. Convinced that Hitler would not negotiate in good faith, Britain, feeling sufficiently prepared to go to war if necessary, and France formerly guaranteed Poland's integrity and independence. The following month Hitler renounced the German–Polish Non-Aggression Pact. In anticipation of settling the 'Polish Question' in Germany's favour, on 23 August 1939, Germany and the Soviet Union signed secret protocols to their own non-aggression pact detailing their respective division of Poland and the Baltic States.

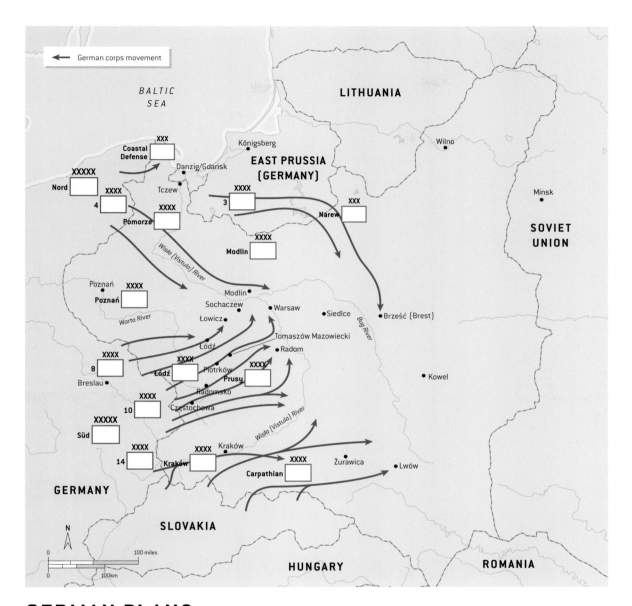

GERMAN PLANS

To eliminate the possibility of a two-front war, Hitler's forces would need to conduct a rapid campaign against Poland in order to reinforce Germany's weakened western border as soon as possible. On 25 August Germany's OKW (Oberkommando der Wehrmacht, or 'High Command of the Armed Forces') issued orders for 'Case White', the invasion plan for Poland, although negotiations between Hitler and Mussolini proceeded poorly; the orders were rescinded, but not all units received them in time, and some temporary border incidents ensued.

In Rundstedt's centre, General der Artillerie Walter von Reichenau's 10. Armee was to defeat Lódź Army, secure crossings over the Wisła River, some 300km to the north-east,

1. Panzer-Division

Generalleutnant Rudolf Schmidt; 11,792 and 308 tanks (including 122 PzKpfw II)*

PzBrig 1 (Generalmajor Josef Harpe Schaal): PzRgt 1 (Oberstleutnant Johannes Nedtwig); PzRgt 2 (Oberstleutnant Karl Keltsch)

1. SchtzBrig (Generalmajor Friedrich Kirchner): SchtzRgt 1; KBtl 1

AR 73; AufklAbt (mot.) 4; PzAbAbt 37; PiBtl 37; NachAbt 37

4. Panzer-Division

Generalmajor Georg-Hans Reinhardt; 10,286 and 295 tanks (including 130 PzKpfw II)*

PzBrig 5 (Generalmajor Max von Hartlieb-Walsporn): PzRgt 35 (Oberstleutnant Heinrich Eberbach); PzRgt 36 (Oberst Hermann Breith)

SchtzRgt 12**; AR 103; AufklAbt (mot.) 7; PzAbAbt 49; PiBtl 79; NachAbt 79

*Indicates the actual number of Panzers available on 1 September 1939.

**There was no *Schützen-Brigade* structure in this division during the Polish campaign.

1. leichte Division (mot.)

Generalmajor Friedrich-Wilhelm von Loeper; 10,418 and 227 tanks (including 65 PzKpfw II)

PzRgt 11; KavSchtzRgt 4; AR 76 (mot.); KAbt 6; AufklAbt (mot.) 6; PzAbAbt 41; PiBtl 57; NachAbt 82

and strike Warsaw. Tasked with leading this effort, General der Kavallerie Erich Hoepner's XVI. Armeekorps (mot.) included Generalleutnant Rudolf Schmidt's 1. Panzer-Division and Generalmajor Georg-Hans Reinhardt's 4. Panzer-Division (two of the ten armoured divisions available to the Germans during the campaign), plus 14. Infanterie-Division and 31. Infanterie-Division. Much as Bock's northern prong progressed according to plan, Rundstedt would maintain a rapid tempo, although 14. Armee initially struggled to pass through the few crossings through the Carpathian Mountains. The more open terrain before 10. Armee and 8. Armee, however, would enable greater manoeuvrability, with the latter army having an intentional hanging left flank to allow it to consolidate its forces along the primary axis of advance, and avoid dispersing its formations along a lengthy frontage, as Poznań Army would soon be cut off and eliminated.

POLISH PLANS

To address a potential invasion, the Polskie Sily Zbrojne (Polish Armed Forces) were allocated frontier defensive zones, with wargames and strategic planning simulating invasions from Germany, or from the Soviet Union, or both. In each scenario, French and Romanian support remained a key component to battlefield success; the Poles factored in their allies' rapid response, as part of a strategy to force Germany into the undesirable position of fighting a war on two fronts. Reciprocally, this would enable Poland to better distribute or position its forces to address threats from other areas.

During mobilization as part of Plan 'Z' (Zachod/West), Polish formations were activated rather piecemeal following the German annexation of what remained of Czechoslovakia in March 1939. By that time the Polish High Command anticipated a potential German invasion force equating to some 70 divisions, to which they

PzKpfw II tanks roll into Poland, 1 September 1939. Of the 18 *Armeekorps* fielded by the Germans, seven contained armoured elements, which were allocated to every army except 8. Armee. Each of these seven corps employed armoured and/or motorized division-sized, ad hoc *Kampfgruppe* spearheads that included artillery, infantry, anti-tank, *Pionier* (combat engineer) and other supporting assets, which as an integrated team possessed the strength, flexibility and stamina to penetrate an adversary's echeloned defences along a limited frontage, attack their command, control and logistics, and produce a rapid battlefield tempo that was difficult to counter. As 1. Panzer-Division and 4. Panzer-Division struck for the boundary between Łódź Army and Kraków Army, the tankers had excellent morale, considering their formations respectively possessed 309 and 341 tanks, mostly PzKpfw I and II. To compensate for a shortage of domestic vehicles, the Germans incorporated some 16,000 appropriated civilian vehicles from Austria and the former Czechoslovakia for the campaign. While initially useful, such substitutes lacked the necessary robustness for combat, and due to their great variety, made logistics and maintenance a challenge. (Pictorial Parade/Getty Images)

decided the best solution was to split their forces into northern and southern operational groups. Considering western Poland protruded into Germany, and was surrounded on three sides, this division accommodated for the relatively untenable territory, while remaining far enough forwards to present an effective defence, and trading space for time. Each Polish army was to cover up to a 200km front with its subordinate infantry divisions each occupying between 12km to 25km of front, depending upon terrain and enemy movements. The main defensive belt would be 2km deep with a conventional linear defence. The cavalry would provide scouting and act as a mobile defence for up to 9km in front as a screen to the main defences, while infantry formations remained in more fixed, fortified positions, as part of the main line of resistance. Artillery was normally up to 3km behind the main defensive line to provide support, and better adapt to fluid situations. Larger cities near the border provided their own battalion-sized formations, which would defend regional assets of import, with the Polish Air Force and the motorized assets providing support.

By late August 1939, Poland began secretly mobilizing its Army to 700,000 strong, with many military, civilian and religious authorities professing the nation's assured battlefield ascendancy over the Germans. With a general mobilization ordered on 29 August, cancelled at Britain's request, and then re-ordered the following day, only 70 per cent of planned strength was available to counter the invasion. For the still-forming Prusy Army, only 15 of 63 expected battalions and 21 of 119 AFVs (including armoured cars) were available on 1 September. The front-line Łódź Army was naturally in better shape, with 35 of 54 battalions and 73 of 107 AFVs fielded. Tactically, decisions stipulated employing night fighting and improvisation to fight a superior force, but against fast-moving armoured and motorized formations, such an approach was a temporary solution at best, and not suited to maintaining an orderly, co-ordinated operational withdrawal. Łódź Army's commander, Major-General Juliusz Rómmel, was to defend the area within Łódź, Piotrków and the border, while also maintaining contact with his neighbouring formations, especially the exposed Poznań Army to the north-west. To accomplish this task, he respectively deployed 10th and 28th Infantry divisions along the Warta River's west bank, while

A single-turret 7TP in Czeski Cieszyn. (Keystone-France/ Gamma-Keystone via Getty Images)

30th Infantry Division was placed along his left near Kłobuck, along with Wołyńska Cavalry Brigade and 7th Infantry Division. Further back, 2nd Legions Infantry Division and Kresowa Cavalry Brigade established themselves near Bełchatów and Zduńska Wola, respectively.

On 30 August, Marshal Edward Śmigły-Rydz put Poland on a war footing, but general mobilization had to be delayed in order to meet agreements with Britain and France to avoid inflaming the diplomatically tense situation, as such an action could be judged an act of war by international standards. With war imminent, on 31 August, the Polish Air Force was ordered to disperse to secret airfields. Believing Britain and France would adhere to their agreement to act within two weeks of the Germans crossing the border; Śmigły-Rydz formulated a strategy of delaying actions until his allies attacked western Germany, thereby enabling a decisive Polish counter-attack reminiscent of the defence of Warsaw in 1920. Śmigły-Rydz, however, neglected to consider Soviet intervention.

COMBAT

BEYOND MOKRA

While 4. Panzer-Division struggled to push beyond the Mokra sector and cross the Liswarta River, by 2 September 1. Panzer-Division had advanced north-east of Kłobuck. Having suffered unexpectedly heavy casualties, many German formations began using infantry to lead an attack, as they were better suited across various terrain types, with armour and artillery in support. Compared to the previous day's fight around Mokra, 4. Panzer-Division began a much more co-ordinated and prepared attack, which moved methodically forwards as artillery helped soften Polish resistance.

A Polish 37mm anti-tank gun, rolled over and destroyed by German armour during the battle of the Tuchola Forest near the village of Grupa in the Polish Corridor. (© IWM MH 18234)

Having recently advanced to within 110km of OG Piotrków, 2nd LTB received additional ammunition in Gałków. Obeying Łódź Army's order, at around 1430hrs on 2 September, Karpow prepared to move towards Kamieńsk and Radomsko, where he was to join Wołyńska Cavalry Brigade, which acted as OG Piotrków's mobile reserve. At 1600hrs SchtzRgt 12 set off for its next objective, some 20km away and west of Kruszyna, which it reached at midnight after travelling through sandy, marshy terrain. After a short rest the German motorized infantrymen continued towards the Warta River 8km to the north, and forced the Widawka River. During the night, active patrols from both sides skirmished along both sides of the Warta River.

By 1100hrs on 3 September, spearheads of 1. Panzer-Division and 4. Panzer-Division had cleared the Warta River and renewed their advance north, their rapid progress creating confusion for Polish command and control. With the immediate German threat focusing on the area between the Warta and Piotrków, the armour commander for Łódź Army, Colonel Stanisław Rola-Arciszewski, again redirected 2nd LTB. The unnecessary movement hindered 2nd LTB's timely deployment and wasted precious fuel, as the unit now moved to a forest near Korszew, 5km east of Bełchatów, where it was assigned to 2nd Legions Infantry Division, part of OG Piotrków. With a British and French ultimatum calling for the cessation of combat operations in Poland having expired, both countries declared war, as did Australia, New Zealand and India. Considering the rapid German advance into Poland, the time it would take to mobilize, and a lack of desire to pursue intervention aggressively, the measure was a symbolic empty gesture, as Poland would undoubtedly fall before it could be effectively enacted.

After crossing the Widawka River, 1. Panzer-Division turned towards the north-east for Przedbórz on the Pilica River, and diverged from 4. Panzer-Division's axis of attack, but their depleted, exhausted adversary proved unable to exploit the gap. As he had little professional military knowledge, and no War College instruction, Major-General Stefan Dąb-Biernacki's advancement to command Prusy Army resulted from his having been part of Piłsudski's inner circle. Not surprisingly, his indecision resulted in contact between Łódź and Kraków armies being severed, and Wołyńska Cavalry Brigade was forced to fall back on Kaliska. To plug the gap, Rómmel had inserted 2nd Legions Infantry Division as a stopgap between Kamieńsk and Piotrków, with 7th HMG Battalion as support. After three days of often frustrating fighting, and heavy losses in men and equipment, the Germans had pushed to within a day's march to Piotrków, and prepared to fight the deciding breakthrough battle in the Góry Borowskie Hills – the key to the Polish defence in the area.

THE GÓRY BOROWSKIE HILLS

On the morning of 4 September, OG Kruszewski, Prusy Army's northern group, tried to move from Tomaszów Mazowiecki towards Piotrków behind the relatively weak defence organized the previous day between Bełchatów and Rozprza. Considering the coming counter-attack's importance, Brigadier-General Jan Kuszewski's superior, Dąb-Biernacki, assumed direct control. With 4. Panzer-Division spearheads moving up along the left rear of 1. Panzer-Division, 31. Infanterie-Division emerged from its reserve status, but struggled to advance along the main road to Bełchatów. As elements of

PzRgt 1 approached Polish positions near Rozprza around noon, they confronted 146th Infantry Regiment, which blocked the direct approach to the town, and the low, swampy terrain surrounding the Prudka Creek and Łucyna River prevented a quick flanking assault. German artillery fired on the town, and the village of Jeżów just upstream. At 1500hrs, elements of 4. Panzer-Division attacked into the wooded terrain of Góry Borowskie, but heavy resistance forced them to pull back to regroup, with fighting lasting until darkness. Confident that he could counter Wołyńska Cavalry Brigade along his right, Schmidt continued to manoeuvre towards Piotrków, amid frequent Polish air attacks. A few kilometres to the north-west at Wygoda, 2/2nd LTB waited in an ambush position in the thick woods along one of the two main routes from Częstochowa to Piotrków. Eating a lunch of biscuits and preserves, the Polish tankers looked out across the flat, largely open ground to the south at SchtzRgt 1's growing dust cloud. Soon after, lead German armoured cars passed through Laski and halted before a destroyed bridge over the Prudka Creek. As several German crewmen dismounted to examine the situation and determine how to cross the surrounding marshy terrain, 3/7th HMG Battalion and an artillery platoon waited on the opposite bank around the grounds of the Jeżów Mansion.

Understanding the critical situation on his left, and the threat of the Germans capturing Piotrków – thereby benefitting their own logistics to his detriment – at 1335hrs Thommée committed his rearguard to a counter-attack. With support from 11th Infantry Battalion and other elements of Wołyńska Cavalry Brigade, 2nd LTB's 47 tanks would strike from their forest positions near Karczew. At 1400hrs, after receiving an order near Bogdanów, 1/2nd LTB moved into the forest near Wola Krzysztoporska to defend the Prudka Creek, where personnel of II./SchtzRgt 1 struggled to fashion a crossing while subjected to Polish machine-gun and artillery fire. An hour later, 2/2nd LTB and 3/2nd LTB were ordered to a forested area some 4km away as a reserve, but before they arrived, two platoons from 1/2nd LTB sallied from Wola Krzysztoporska to rebuff a German armoured-car patrol, destroying two vehicles.

To quell the Polish tankers, and secure a foothold on the Prudka Creek's northern bank, 6./PzPgt 1 and a motorized-infantry company from 1. Panzer-Division responded. Without immediate artillery support, and recalling their recent experiences in the face of Polish anti-tank guns, the German tank crews cautiously approached their objective beyond the creek. Like much of the terrain from the German border, the Góry Borowskie Hills contained numerous woods and copses, and the Polish defenders

These single-turret 7TPs are being inspected in April 1939. While the PzKpfw I lacked any real chance of destroying a 7TP at any range, and had armour that was barely able to stop rifle and machine-gun rounds, the PzKpfw II needed to be within around 250m of the 7TP for the German tank's main armament to be effective. Reciprocally, the 7TP could destroy both German tanks at ranges of up to 1,800m and 1,500m, respectively. (Popperfoto/Getty Images)

would use them to great advantage to harry and delay their adversary. 7TPs deployed in the forest, with large intervals – at least 50m – between vehicles, as the Germans advanced in several clusters across largely open terrain.

Corpses of both sides littered the ground before 1/2nd LTB's position, as its 7TPs frantically engaged targets as soon as they acquired them. The noise, smoke and confusion of combat hindered communication, but had little effect on the Poles' accuracy, as they were on the defensive and largely hidden from the Germans' direct view. The German armoured fighting vehicles returned fire with equal haste, but finding the camouflaged Polish targets proved frustrating. Polish artillery fire destroyed two Panzers and caused considerable confusion for the attackers, who soon withdrew. In their place, a second *Kampfgruppe* comprised of 7./PzRgt 1 and 8./PzRgt 1 manoeuvred towards the defenders' left flank to eliminate the pesky Polish artillery. After receiving a gruff radio order to engage the new German threat, the 7TPs moved down the Prudka Creek to make contact. The Poles attacked once again; as the 7TPs got into range, they opened up with 37mm cannon and machine guns. Although the PzKpfw II tanks returned fire, the Polish tankers soon destroyed at least three PzKpfw I and a PzKpfw II, for the loss of a single 7TP and half-a-dozen men wounded.

Too late to support the second armoured assault, German artillery finally began shelling 1/2nd LTB's position. This German fire, along with Luftwaffe support, forced the defenders to withdraw to their wooded starting point, taking two damaged 7TPs with them to be repaired. The German bombardment intensified, and huge, ancient oak trees were destroyed, spraying jagged splinters, alongside erupting earth and clouds of black or grey smoke and dust. From there 1/2nd LTB continued through the woods, past Wygoda, and soon arrived at the village of Wola Krzysztoporska. With the Germans apparently unaware that the Polish tank force had vacated the area, the German bombing continued for the next half-hour, until Polish PZL.23 *Karaś* light bombers attacked the German armoured vehicles.

Quiet soon descended across 1/2nd LTB's front, save for the occasional gunshot, as exhausted Polish infantry remnants from 2nd Legions Infantry Division limped rearwards. Believing the Poles had abandoned the Jeżów area, several *Panzerspähwagen* cautiously returned to the destroyed bridge and were left unaccosted for the moment. The Polish tankers waited, however, with one platoon just off the Gorzkowice–Piotrków highway, as the lead German vehicles approached to some 150m. Radio orders among 'Lynx', 'Wildcat', and similar call-signs prompted the 7TP tanks into action, with their 37mm anti-tank rounds producing a purplish streak of smoke on leaving the barrel and an occasional bluish flash on impact. Inside the Polish tanks, noxious fumes made the already cramped interiors even more uncomfortable. The platoon was subsequently ordered forwards into a furious exchange of fire, with many tanks purposely driving over German infantrymen.

At 1700hrs, I./SchtzRgt 12 probes began advancing over the Prudka Creek towards Jeżów. In response, 1/2nd LTB and 2/2nd LTB set out from Wola Krzysztoporska and headed south through the Wygoda Woods. While 1/2nd LTB moved towards the Prudka Creek crossing, Captain Konstantego Hajdenki's 2/2nd LTB set out for the high ground near Magdalenka. Seeing an opportunity to strike, they engaged their adversaries at Jeżów, destroying three German tanks and damaging a fourth for the loss of one 7TP destroyed and two damaged. 2/2nd LTB and an equivalent infantry formation attacked German positions at the Wygoda Woods at 1800hrs. Although these actions were intended to keep the Germans from crossing the Prudka Creek, 2nd LTB had to withdraw that evening, as Thommée had no immediate reserves to commit to support them. German forces subsequently occupied the vacated positions, including the Wygoda Woods, and after darkness the villages of Siomki, Krzyżanów and Cekanów. Several Panzers became stuck in the marshy terrain, with 1/2nd LTB withdrawing to a spot near Bogdanów for much-needed repairs to the company's battle-scarred 7TPs.

At 1830hrs, the Germans grouped some 60 tanks of II./PzRgt 1 – including 20 PzKpfw I and 28 PzKpfw II – supported by SchtzRgt 1, I./AR 73 and II./AR 93, and moved to attack 2nd Legions Infantry Regiment. Over the next hour or so, the German assault was broken by Polish fire from a variety of machine guns, mortars and anti-tank guns. 4. Panzer-Division subsequently withdrew to near Parzniewice, in the centre of the Góry Borowskie Hills positions, and ceased fighting for the night. The defenders, however, mounted a four-company raid armed with grenades and petrol bottles. German security uncovered the Polish activity, and with the subsequent arrival of infantry and armour elements, the Germans drove off the Polish counter-attack. Polish artillery responded and forced the Germans located around Parzniewice to pull back and regroup. After dark, SchtzRgt 1 pulled back from Laski and established a bridgehead at Jeżów, 1km to the east.

Two PzKpfw II Ausf A tanks (221 and 541) and a PzKpfw IV Ausf B or C (811) from PzRgt 1 that were destroyed near Ruszki–Kiernozia on 16 September 1939, during the battle of Bzura. Deemed salvageable, these vehicles were transported to a collection point near a water tower in southern Sochaczew. (Christian Ankerstjerne)

TO PIOTRKÓW

As dawn arrived at 0453hrs on 5 September, 14. Infanterie-Division, anchoring the right of XVI. Armeekorps (mot.), prepared to contain Wołyńska Cavalry Brigade in the Lubién Forest, south-east of Piotrków. With that sector relatively stable, 1. Panzer-Division and 4. Panzer-Division began an offensive to capture the city, the former mounting a direct assault while the latter undertook a flanking thrust to Piotrków's west and north; 31. Infanterie-Division acted as corps reserve. At 0545hrs, heavy German artillery fire and Luftwaffe bombing struck Polish forces along the Góry Borowskie Hills to facilitate the coming ground offensive.

At 0800hrs a messenger from the adjacent 2nd Legions Infantry Regiment picked up Karpow and drove him to his commander, Colonel Ludwik Czyżewski, to receive new orders. En route, a nearby battery from Wołyńska Cavalry Brigade nearly opened fire on Karpow's party, having initially mistaken it for a German reconnaissance patrol. By 0915hrs Czyżewski and Karpow had formulated an attack plan that was to commence at 1030hrs. To best counter the German advance, Thommée ordered 2nd

On 5 September SchtzRgt 1 pushed into Piotrków from the south, including Bujny, while 4. Panzer-Division flanked the area to the north before continuing towards Tomaszów Mazowiecki. While 2nd LTB withdrew from its aborted counter-attack just to the west, the German thrust directly at Piotrków pushed through dissolving Polish positions, and against II/19th Artillery and flanking elements of 86th Infantry Regiment (both of 19th Infantry Division). Taken in June, this view towards the south-east shows low hills that enabled movement while relatively concealed from enemy ground forces. As the Germans increasingly possessed control of the air, Polish units were unable to make effective use of such open areas, and gravitated to the region's numerous copses and forests to regroup, rest and fight. Forced to conduct much of their movement at night, the Poles found that their strained logistics system, inaccurate intelligence and reactive command and control conspired to erode their ability to resist effectively. (Artur Popiołek)

OPPOSITE Having advanced over 100km in four days, 1. Panzer-Division and 4. Panzer-Division prepared to secure the important road hub at Piotrków, which would facilitate a steady logistics flow as the formations continued their advance on Warsaw. With 1st LTB finally in a position to contribute to the Polish fighting operational withdrawal, on 5 September its three companies launched a counter-attack from the Krezna and Wygoda against German positions along the Prudka River. Although locally successful, German momentum, and an increasingly fragmented Polish defence, meant the latter was soon forced to continue falling back toward Warsaw and abandon Piotrków to its fate.

LTB and Wołyńska Cavalry Brigade's 11th Infantry Battalion – the latter as it was immediately available – to strike 1. Panzer-Division's left. To do so, the Poles would deploy their forces in two battlegroups that had been reorganized during the night, and make for Jeżów and the northern bank of the Prudka Creek. With 19th Infantry Division blocking 1. Panzer-Division's direct route towards Piotrków, the Polish tankers' operation was intended to keep Schmidt's assault off balance by cutting the Jeżów–Piotrków road, interfering with his ability to co-ordinate with 4. Panzer-Division and enabling Polish infantry reinforcements to secure the recaptured ground.

Pre-empting the Polish assault, ahead of the general German advance a column of two Panzers, eight armoured cars and six infantry-laden trucks suddenly arrived before 2/2nd LTB's concealed position in the woods near Wola Krzysztoporska. Hajdenki quickly responded by having his 7TPs engage the surprised Germans. With four tanks from one platoon providing covering fire, the remaining two Polish platoons attacked the German probe, which quickly headed for the relative safety of the surrounding field's undulating terrain. Meanwhile, out of range for direct intervention on the north-eastern side of Piotrków, 1st LTB established a position around Sulejów, in order to support friendly formations in that sector in a bid to resist the anticipated German assault on the key road hub.

As 4. Panzer-Division pushed north between Bełchatów and Piotrków, to its right, 1. Panzer-Division's previous success north of Laski and Rozprza had extended its Prudka Creek bridgehead to some 4km and east to the Lubién Forest, and had left the German formation in an excellent position from which to continue its advance. Having had time to consolidate, the remainder of XVI. Armeekorps (mot.) crashed through the inconsistent Polish defences, causing chaos and confusion, as weaker sections gave way and exposed those Polish forces that remained to being outflanked. At 1000hrs the villages of Laski and Wola Rokszyca were hit by heavy German fire in preparation for ground forces moving through these areas. Along 2nd LTB's left, 11th Infantry Battalion, backed by an artillery battery, supported part of 2/2nd LTB as it set out from Krężną and struck through Wola Krzysztoporska, using the hilly terrain west of the Prudka Creek as a screen. At 1030hrs, Second Lieutenant (res.) Wacław Zarugiewicz's 3rd Platoon, 1/2nd LTB advanced on the left, with 37mm Bofors guns from an anti-tank platoon of Wołyńska Cavalry Brigade some 300m away providing support. Soon after, lead elements of I./PzRgt 1 moved to within some

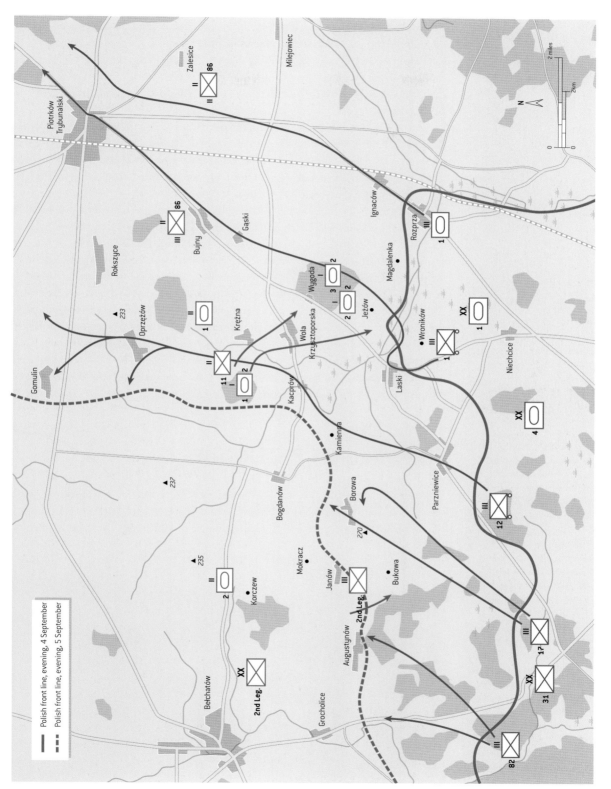

Polish front line, evening, 4 September

Polish front line, evening, 5 September

500m, at which point Zarugiewicz's 7TPs conducted accurate fire into the German armoured advance, which left several tanks burning and prompted the remainder to seek cover in the Wygoda Woods. At ranges of 500m or less, the Polish 37mm gun could penetrate roughly 48mm of armour, while the PzKpfw II's 2cm main armament could achieve only 14mm. To get the vanguard moving, German artillery targeted 2nd LTB's elements.

The remainder of the unit, 1/2nd LTB and 2/2nd LTB, advanced towards Siomki and Kisiele at either end of the Wygoda Woods. At 1100hrs, 1/2nd LTB reached Jeżów, where it proceeded to destroy 11 German tanks and enabled the capture of 70 German soldiers. By noon the surrounding situation had become dire for the German defenders. Just across the Prudka Creek, I./SchtzRgt 12 bore the brunt of the Polish advance; backed by I./AR 103, the German motorized infantrymen successfully maintained their position. Although 2nd LTB had initially achieved surprise, its effort came to naught, as it ran into the obscured positions of PzAbAbt 37 just inside the Wygoda Woods and was engaged with close-range fire from its 3.7cm guns. With the Polish assault halted, I./SchtzRgt 1 struck 2/2nd LTB's left flank; this attack, along with fire from II./AR 73, prompted Karpow to withdraw his unit, along with the battered 11th Infantry Battalion. Over the last two days, Karpow's command had destroyed 17 Panzers, two self-propelled guns and 14 armoured cars, and even though the losses he incurred were proportionately much less, dwindling logistics and the fact that the Germans usually occupied the battlefield after combat had ended meant immobilized Polish tanks and damaged equipment were increasingly left behind. It was the last large-scale tank engagement of the campaign and the final time 2nd LTB fought as a complete unit.

THE FALL OF PIOTRKÓW

Throughout 6 September, Prusy Army and Łódź Army were in retreat, due in large measure to Dąb-Biernacki's inability to formulate an effective response; 4. Panzer-Division and 1. Panzer-Division were striking between them in order to disrupt

Single-turret 7TP tanks on manoeuvres during April 1939. Having lost four 7TPs on 5 September, Karpow's Polish tankers made their way back to Wola Krzysztoporska, where fear of a low-flying German reconnaissance aircraft temporarily kept them from continuing towards Krężną. Setting off across the region's undulating hills and numerous wooded areas, 2nd LTB's remnants, including two-dozen 7TPs (six of which were damaged), set off in three ragged companies separated from each other by up to 300m. As Polish tanks tended to fight individually, or in small groups, greater German numbers provided the ability to contain them, and the 7TPs could have little effect on larger operations. (Popperfoto/Getty Images)

command and control, as well as the formation of reserves, and better penetrate into the Poles' rear areas. 1. Panzer-Division moved along the Łucyna River towards Milejowiec, where it attacked a stubborn 19th Infantry Division that returned the favour with its own counter-attack. German armoured formations, with their greater depth of resources, were increasingly able to uncover weak sections in the Polish defences and could more quickly redirect additional forces to exploit a penetration before the Poles could counter it. Such tactical successes had a cumulative operational effect that provided momentum to the Germans, which allowed them to compensate more easily for any battlefield setbacks that arose. The Polish defence was increasingly disorderly, which ultimately resulted in Wołyńska Cavalry Brigade remaining in the Lubién Forest and the Germans were able to defeat three Polish infantry divisions individually. By 1600hrs, 4. Panzer-Division had crushed 19th Infantry Division, and within an hour, vanguard elements of 1. Panzer-Division had bypassed Piotrków in an anti-clockwise movement, and – with assistance from tactical air support – approached the forests to the city's north-east. To the east, PzRgt 2 pushed ahead to make contact and encircle its prize, before continuing 10km to the north-east to capture Wolbórz en route to the Polish capital. By 1730hrs, the Germans had captured Piotrków proper, but with sporadic urban resistance continuing, I./SchtzRgt 1 secured the area later that night. Two hours later, Piotrków fell to the Germans.

With its adversaries disintegrating as they fell back towards Warsaw, 4. Panzer-Division exploited the situation by pressing for Tomaszów Mazowiecki and sought to assault the worn-out 13th Infantry Division. Having captured thousands of prisoners from 19th Infantry Division's remains – including its commander – part of the German spearhead was diverted to process the haul. During the night 29th Infantry Division launched several unco-ordinated, piecemeal counter-attacks on the flank of the German penetration to restrain it, with little result save heavy Polish casualties. East of the Wolbórz–Będków line, PzRgt 36 broke the newly formed Polish front and by dusk had extended an armoured wedge towards Cekanów. AufklAbt (mot.) 7 covered PzRgt 36's left towards the north-west from Będków, while I./SchtzRgt 12 followed to establish a position to the left of the Będków–Lubochnia highway. II./PzRgt 35 assumed all-round positions due west of Rudnik, while I./PzRgt 35 remained in nearby Bieżywody. Around midnight 1. Panzer-Division secured Wolbórz and established a bridgehead over the Wolbórka, some 20km from Prusy Army's headquarters at Spala, near the Wolbórka's confluence with the Pilica River just east of Tomaszów Mazowiecki. With the speed of the Germans' seemingly inexorable advance from the north and south-west of the capital having come as a shock to the Polish defenders, earlier on 6 September the Polish General Staff had abandoned Warsaw.

On 6 September, Prusy Army withdrew through the Sulejów area east of Piotrków, in an effort to avoid vanguard elements of 1. Panzer-Division and 4. Panzer-Division as they moved towards Tomaszów Mazowiecki. With 14. Infanterie-Division covering the Polish right flank near Lubién, the German armoured thrust split 30th and 13th Infantry divisions, which along with other disrupted Polish formations were faced with a choice between mounting a piecemeal defence that threatened encirclement and destruction, or falling back on the relative safety of the capital and Wisła River while dissolving into what were increasingly unco-ordinated, ad hoc elements. As most rivers and creeks between Tomaszów Mazowiecki and Warsaw ran along the axis of the Polish withdrawal, German armoured and motorized forces were able to maintain a rapid tempo that within a few days was helping to pin considerable quantities of Polish personnel and equipment around the Bzura River. The view here shows the area around Sulejów in mid-August; Wołyńska Cavalry Brigade would have passed this way during its withdrawal from the Piotrków fighting. (Artur Popiołek)

TOMASZÓW MAZOWIECKI TO THE WISŁA

One week into the campaign, 1. Panzer-Division and 4. Panzer-Division had finally broken through congested Polish front lines around Piotrków and their vanguards now ranged ahead of the remainder of XVI. Armeekorps (mot.). 1. Panzer-Division had pushed elements as far north as Rawa Mazowiecka, with 4. Panzer-Division not far off its left flank, around Brzeziny. By 8 September, Schmidt directed his armoured and motorized formations directly at the Polish capital, while to his left, vanguard elements of PzRgt 35 captured Raszyn, although they were subsequently halted before Warsaw's incomplete defences. As three PzKpfw II attempted to storm a barricade at Warsaw's Narutowicza Square, 7TPs from the city's mobile defence force disabled one and dispersed its companions.

Ordered up from nearby Drzewiczka for support, Captain Marian Górski's 2/1st LTB destroyed or immobilized seven more Panzers and dispersed the accompanying German motorized infantry, at the cost of three 7TPs. With 1. Panzer-Division pushing beyond Tomaszów Mazowiecki for Warsaw, the additional threat from the approaching 13. Infanterie-Division (mot.) meant that 1st LTB could not remain in the area for long. Already, German artillery fire was falling around the Drzewiczka River, a tributary of the Pilica, in support of reconnaissance units probing north of Opoczno. As refugees continued to flood through the area, during the afternoon 7TPs destroyed a pair of German armoured cars of AufklAbt 13. An hour later two more such vehicles arrived and although they entered a cemetery to avoid the Polish tanks, the 7TPs destroyed them as well.

With 13th Infantry Division having broken and disintegrated over the past day, 1st LTB was tasked with providing a rearguard around Odrzywół. Having pulled back 25km from its positions near Sulejów, during the morning of 8 September the battalion was ordered to strengthen the defences along the Drzewiczka, much to the consternation of its commander, Major Adam Kubin. Allocated as dispersed platoons, or even individual vehicles, the tanks of 1/1st LTB operated around the Pilica crossing at Nowe Miasto. When approaching the crossing in Odrzywół German artillery from 13. Infanterie-Division (mot.) advancing from the south targeted 1/1st LTB. During the engagement, the Polish tankers destroyed three PzKpfw II and a PzKpfw 35(t) from PzRgt 11, a unit of 1. leichte Division that had been temporarily reallocated to 13. Infantry Division (mot.), for the loss of two Polish tanks.

By the afternoon of 8 September a general Polish retreat was in effect, with the area's narrow forest roads hindering movement and co-ordination. With the inexorable German advance not far behind, that evening 1st LTB and its 24 remaining 7TPs withdrew eastwards to Jedlińsk along the Radom–Warsaw highway. In the chaos, communication between the battalion and its Technical-Logistics Company was lost, and repairing damaged or disabled tanks became nearly impossible. Owing to limited fuel supplies and in an act of desperation to keep their vehicles in operation, many 7TP commanders resorted to siphoning diesel from other vehicles and appropriating civilian kerosene as a substitute. Although the latter burned hotter and lowered lubricity, it did not adversely affect engine performance – especially as the tanks' life expectancy could now be measured in days.

In line with Rómmel's orders, withdrawing Polish forces were to cross the Wisła River, where they were to be reorganized along this formidable barrier. First Lieutenant Andrzej Chołoniewski of 2nd Platoon, 3/2nd LTB later recalled that having done so, he received orders from Captain Antoni Próchniewicz, the commander of 1/2nd LTB, to relocate 80km south-east of the capital at Żelechów, but the message was unsubstantiated, and no one was there on arrival at Żelechów the next day. With its communications with Prusy Army headquarters similarly disrupted, 1st LTB continued on, often using functioning 7TPs to tow their disabled brethren to cannibalize for spare parts, a problem compounded by the loss of numerous maintenance personnel from the workshop in the rush to effect a crossing.

TOWARDS WARSAW

As 4. Armee and 8. Armee steadily constricted Poznań Army and Pomorze Army from the north and south, respectively, as they fell back on Inowrocław and Warsaw, the Poles' ability to reorganize and resupply was continually hindered as they proved unable to stabilize their front and offer effective resistance for more than short periods. German intelligence and reconnaissance, however, proved unable to piece together the developing situation quickly enough and presented the Poles with an opportunity, which – if successful – would create a large-enough opening for most to get across the Wisła and establish new defences around the capital. Although initially caught flat-footed, German senior commanders possessed greater flexibility and support, and were quick to redeploy nearby formations to help stabilize the situation and eliminate

Polish civilians and soldiers prepare anti-tank defences in Warsaw. On the heels of the Polish High Command, the government had abandoned Warsaw on 7 September. As a token measure, France conducted a plodding 'invasion' of Germany's Saar region, just across the Franco-German border. Unwilling to push more than a few kilometres, the lacklustre French effort initiated what would soon be coined the 'Phoney War', in which both sides did little more than watch each other for the next several months.
(© Bettmann/CORBIS)

the Polish break-out. Considerable Luftwaffe support was used to disrupt Polish communications and bomb the ground forces when possible. Fighter support concentrated on the developing pocket, which constricted over the next few days, thereby promoting greater densities of Polish forces and increasing the destruction wrought from the air. The Polish forces on the ground had few resources to counter such attacks, save some dedicated anti-aircraft weapons and rifles.

With the bulk of 1. Panzer-Division having moved up to probe Warsaw's southern edge, 1st LTB continued to look for a way to reach the Polish capital, which acted as a magnet for the numerous Polish formations that had lost contact with higher commands. Having lost ten 7TPs, with five of these being abandoned in the darkness as their crews were unable to perform necessary repairs, 1st LTB provided support for a Polish infantry assault near Głowaczów on 9 September, where many foot-soldiers rode 7TPs into the fight. Although two Polish tanks bogged down in marshy terrain, the remainder assaulted positions at Głowaczów defended by elements of 1. leichte Division. The Poles destroyed a PzKpfw 38(t) and a PzKpfw IV Ausf B of PzRgt 25, and alongside elements of 13th Infantry Division pushed the Germans back, allowing numerous Polish forces to escape to the north-east, although at a cost of six 7TPs destroyed in the effort. Following the Głowaczów fight, seven 7TPs from 2/1st LTB co-ordinated with elements of 13th Infantry Division and helped them fight their way through German forces that blocked the direct route across the Wisła River near Ryczywołu. Although friendly forces across the waterway attempted to send badly needed fuel to the Poles on the left bank across a ford, the effort failed. With no hope of conducting an effective fight, the Polish tank crews drove their mounts into the river, crossed over, and continued north, while a *Kampfgruppe* from 1. leichte Division secured an undamaged bridge over the Wisła at Świerże Górne. 1st LTB's surviving 7TPs managed to retreat over the Wisła, and made for nearby Garwolin. Running low on fuel, and with no more than 20 depleted 7TPs remaining, 1st LTB dispersed near the town on 10 September. 14 tanks eventually reached Brześć over the next few days, where they received badly needed maintenance and resupply before turning south.

With PzRgt 35 having been pulled from Warsaw's western suburbs at 1100hrs on 9 September and sent to help contain the growing Polish pocket along the Bzura, one *Kampfgruppe* from 4. Panzer-Division (Infanterie-Regiment (mot.) *Leibstandarte-SS Adolf Hitler*, I./PzRgt 36 and AR 103) pushed west to establish a new defensive position, while a second (the remainder of PzBrig 5 and SchtzRgt 12) worked its way north towards the Wisła at Młociny. At the outset of the campaign, PzRgt 36 had been ordered to keep two *leichte Panzer-Kompanien* – one each from I./PzRgt 36 and II./PzRgt 36 – in Germany as a reserve, leaving each *Panzer-Abteilung* with three companies. That evening, I./PzRgt 36 advanced to the Wawrzyszew District, 5km north-west of the centre of Warsaw, to acquire a better position, when they captured a group of Polish soldiers attempting to get

Built in 1918 and subsequently modernized, armoured train nr. 12 *Poznanczyk* was ordered to defend Warsaw on 5 September 1939. Four days later 4. Panzer-Division cut it off before Błonie, and the train was blown up and abandoned. Here, personnel of *Leibstandarte-SS Adolf Hitler* examine the wreckage. (Library of Congress)

into the Polish capital. Lacking the resources to guard their prisoners, the Germans made them leave their weapons and sent them west towards follow-on units. After sunset a junior officer from PzRgt 36 arrived with 200 prisoners from the west, reporting that unidentified armoured vehicles had been seen entering the nearby Kampinos Woods near Wawrzyszew Cemetery. A platoon from 1./PzRgt 36 was soon sent to investigate what turned out to be 7TPs that had recently served with 2nd LTB, and were now serving with the Dowództwo Obrony Warszawy. Soon after this Polish light-tank platoon crossed the cemetery grounds, the Polish tankers stumbled upon the rear of their German equivalent. Suddenly firing into their midst, the Polish tankers destroyed two Panzers and three accompanying trucks, with one Panzer escaping the action. As part of their haul of weapons, ammunition, petrol and radios, the Polish tankers took several dozen prisoners and recaptured a standard from Ursus Factory that had been a German trophy.

Posted near downtown Warsaw's Krasińscy Gardens, the two 7TP-equipped light-tank companies, and others like them, awaited the inevitable German advance. Having recently fought in Okęcie suburb, on 10 September, 1st LTC suffered heavy losses and its remnants were later merged with 2nd LTC. The latter had started with 11 single-turret 7TPs and participated in a successful defence of the borough of Wola against German infantry and elements of I./PzRgt 35. It was also used for tactical counter attacks, including one around Wawrzyszew on 12 September. Unsuited for urban combat, German tanks were frequently attacked with grenades, Molotov cocktails and explosives that took a heavy toll. On 14 September, much of 4. Panzer-Division was redirected westwards to help contain and destroy Polish forces attempting to break out from their positions between the Bzura and Wisła rivers.

German armour in Poland, 11 September 1939. Four PzKpfw I Ausf B, with a PzKpfw II in the middle, cross what looks to be a partially destroyed stone wall. Likely trying to minimize clustering at an exposed location, they negotiate the obstacle one at a time. (Popperfoto/Getty Images)

STATISTICS AND ANALYSIS

In mid-1939, many European countries – including Poland – lacked recent combat experience and so their recent tank designs remained untried in battle. When the Spanish Civil War began in 1936, Nazi Germany and the Soviet Union had seized the opportunity to field-test new weapon systems and doctrine. During the Spanish

PzKpfw II tanks file past Hitler along the Boulevard Aleje Ujazdowski during the 5 October 1939 victory parade in Warsaw. As these tanks are likely from I./PzRgt 23, and were not committed to combat, it might explain why their white Balkan crosses have not been muted. As an aside, the US and French embassies are out of sight behind the viewer, and just down the block on the right, respectively. (© CORBIS)

conflict it soon became apparent that advances in anti-tank guns meant they could penetrate any armoured target at common engagement ranges. Against an adversary operating from camouflaged positions, a moving tank – hampered by limited visibility, minimal or non-existent inter-vehicle communication and a lack of co-ordination with supporting units – was at a distinct disadvantage. Such tanks would be hard pressed to spot, engage and destroy the enemy before being knocked out or destroyed themselves. Even so, with the fighting in Spain having ended only shortly before the Polish campaign began, tanks such as the PzKpfw II and 7TP had to be employed in combat even though their thin armour had proven a serious liability against contemporary 20mm, 37mm and 45mm armour-piercing projectiles.

PzKpfw II

Senior German commanders such as Guderian and Seeckt had fleshed out an armoured doctrine that emphasized mutually supporting, all-arms formations designed to operate ahead of slower, more cumbersome infantry forces. By stressing concentration of such armoured and motorized forces at key tactical and operational sectors, Guderian's disciples ensured that their less agile adversaries were seldom able to counter the Germans' rapid battlefield tempo for long. During the Spanish Civil War, German advisors and participants had been able to fine-tune existing doctrine based on actual combat, such as adjusting unit type or asset ratios to provide an economy of force, or an optimal administration, support and combat formation. Interaction with aircraft was also paramount to keeping an enemy off-balance, providing localized reconnaissance and ground-target interdiction.

By September 1939 the PzKpfw II was nearing the end of its ability to undertake direct combat roles – the stronger, more powerful PzKpfw III and PzKpfw IV were

A 10.5cm *Wespe* (Wasp) self-propelled gun, based on the PzKpfw II chassis. With little room for the PzKpfw II to evolve as a front-line tank, one option was simply to eliminate the turret and incorporate a larger main gun into an open-top, fixed armoured superstructure. This repurposing extended chassis life, which in the PzKpfw II became the Marder (Martin) II, with a powerful 7.5cm anti-tank gun, and later the *Wespe*. With similar towed guns needing to be transported, and unlimbered and limbered in a relatively time-consuming process that exposed the crew to enemy fire, the tactical benefits of the PzKpfw II variants, and others, was marked. As German industry had not been placed on a total war footing, and AFV expenditures comprised less than 2 per cent of all costs, such expedients proved an inexpensive alternative for captured foreign AFVs as well, although such polyglot groupings, with their various parts and requirements, presented supply and maintenance problems. As a tank, the PzKpfw II progressed through several wartime variants and conversions until production ceased in January 1944. As the PzKpfw II's final purpose-built reconnaissance iteration, the Ausf L *Luchs* (Lynx) had interleaved wheels, and proved effective in its intended role. (Nik Cornish at www.stavka.org.uk)

By 1941, the PzKpfw II was unsuited for front-line combat and was instead used for peripheral tasks such as reconnaissance. The accelerated crucible of armoured combat on the Eastern Front from 1941 would result in progressively larger and more powerful tanks, culminating in the Tiger II, which was over seven times heavier than the PzKpfw II and possessed up to 180mm of armour protection backed by a high-velocity 8.8cm main gun. Here, a PzKpfw II Ausf F tows a captured Soviet ZiS-5 4×2 cargo truck along a typical Russian road. Note the smattering of camouflaging foliage and the 'WH' on the fender for Wehrmacht Heer. (Nik Cornish at www.stavka.org.uk)

envisaged to perform these, but were not available in sufficient quantities. During the Polish campaign the German arsenal contained 3,258 tanks, with the PzKpfw I and PzKpfw II comprising 44 per cent and 38 per cent respectively. Purpose-built main battle tanks such as the PzKpfw III and PzKpfw IV represented just 3 per cent and 6 per cent of the total. With some 250 PzKpfw II knocked out during the fighting, maintenance was found lacking, as was consistent aggressive spirit among the *Panzertruppen*, and thorough reconnaissance.

In combat the PzKpfw II performed adequately considering its thin armour and design as a training vehicle. Its 2cm automatic main armament could engage soft as well as hard targets in up to ten-round bursts, and the tank's relatively small size, and good volume and rate of fire, offered some compensation. The vehicle's good cross-country performance meant it could use movement and terrain to avoid being effectively targeted; its leaf-spring suspension was suited to its light weight and proved to be simple, effective and easy to repair. Although the three-man crew worked within a cramped, non-ergonomic environment, their training promoted teamwork within the vehicle, as well as with other *Kampfgruppe* forces, even though after-action reports from Poland indicated this was often lacking, as was an aggressive spirit. PzKpfw II crews also struggled to maintain fuel and march discipline on campaign, which produced numerous traffic jams that hindered operations. During the Polish campaign, vehicle commanders complained of limited turret visibility, which resulted in a rudimentary cupola being fitted after the conflict ended. As armour protection proved unsatisfactory, additional plate was added to the glacis, which replaced the round front with an angled one.

7TP

In general, the Polish military proved to be unrealistic and over-confident in the years before World War II, placing huge concentrations of troops in the Polish Corridor and remaining ill-equipped to deal with a mechanized war. As light-tank battalions comprised engineers, towed anti-tank and other integrated forces, and support personnel, subordinate elements were potentially available to quickly address unexpected situations. Applied piecemeal in companies and platoons to strengthen threatened sectors, groups of 7TPs often fought in relative isolation and disunity, which was exacerbated by the lack of radios. In less-active defensive operations, such command-and-control deficiencies could be managed. Many officers lacked proper training in how best to employ and support armoured units, and were unfamiliar with using radios as part of their command-and-control repertoire. Maintenance personnel were in short supply, and even though for the campaign's opening two weeks Polish forces fell back on interior lines, congested roadways and disrupted industry conspired with a very short mobilization period to make effective resupply difficult at best. With Polish air assets largely destroyed early, 7TP formations had little chance to affect the operational course of a battle. Like the Polish Army in general, they fought as best they could, with what they had.

Although few in numbers, the 7TP generally proved superior to its PzKpfw II opponent in a direct vehicle comparison. While in a vacuum, both vehicles possessed similar defensive capabilities, with the 7TP's larger cannon and heavier projective permitting greater effective engagement ranges than its adversary. Both vehicles could satisfactorily penetrate the other's plate at average engagement ranges, as each had similar armour protection. Considering the still-developing state of domestic industry, Poland's best fielded production tank was a cost-effective, simple vehicle. Like the PzKpfw II, it lacked the ability to be upgraded or modernized to any worthwhile degree due to its small size that precluded incorporating a larger turret ring, or engine, such as to accommodate for thicker armour plate and increased weight. Its diesel engine proved a logistical handicap, and aside from light enemy tanks and armoured cars it was outclassed on a contemporary battlefield. In an effort to address lessons learned during the Spanish Civil War, development commenced on an improved vehicle with armour sufficient to resist 37mm rounds at ranges greater than 500m. In 1938 PZInż produced 13 such prototypes, but the 9TP would never enter production; examples fought with 2nd LTC in Warsaw. Throughout the Polish campaign, some 70 7TPs (50 per cent) were destroyed in combat, while 13 (10 per cent) broke down or suffered technical problems. A lack of fuel forced 15 (11 per cent) from the fight, with 21 (15 per cent) being surrendered. Of these the Germans captured 20, and the Soviets one, while 20 (14 per cent) entered Romania and were interned.

Following the Polish campaign, the Germans incorporated several captured 7TPs into the *Panzerwaffe*, where they were repainted and marked, and participated in the German victory parade in Warsaw on 8 October. During the subsequent campaign in the West in May 1940, 20 served alongside their former adversaries in 4./PzRgt 1. As the design was increasingly obsolete, the *Beutepanzer* vehicles were usually relegated to police and security personnel in secondary theatres, and performed their final active-service duties in Ukraine and Poland during 1944. Here, a 7TP features on the cover artwork for a book focusing on Ordnungspolizei (regular police) activities during Operation *Barbarossa*. (Public Domain)

AFTERMATH

Seeking to organize Polish defences east of the Wisła River, and hold out until winter, Śmigły-Rydz ordered formations to withdraw towards the more rugged terrain south of Lwów, near the Romanian border. Having relocated his command to Brześć the better to co-ordinate this considerable effort, he assumed the move would buy sufficient time for the Western Allies finally to act decisively, in part as the region south of Lwów contained numerous supply depots, and external resupply was possible via the Danube River and

Polish military personnel cross the Romanian border. On 14 September, Karpow ordered the company-sized remnants of 2nd LTB to make for Kowel; over the next two days, these engaged German armoured spearheads. Fought down, and without fuel, on 17 September the Polish tankers burned their remaining 11 7TPs, made for the Romanian border and eventually crossed into Hungary. Over the next few days, a few Polish formations managed to escape the Bzura Pocket, but the remnants – of what would be the largest Allied counter-offensive until *Barbarossa*, two years later – were destroyed.
(© IWM HU 106377)

10 October 1939: a Soviet BT-7 light tank is pictured at Raków, Poland (now Rakaw, Belarus). (© Bettmann/CORBIS)

Black Sea. Although the Polish Army had suffered a series of devastating operational setbacks, it remained committed to continuing the fight from the south-eastern redoubt.

Turning their attention to eliminate Warsaw, the Germans eased operations in other sectors. As German forces had essentially eliminated the Polish Air Force within the first week, and had pushed their adversaries back onto Warsaw, on 9 September Hitler began redirecting his units westwards to strengthen formations on that front to counter an Allied invasion that was never in the offing – even though they presently fielded 110 divisions in the West to Germany's 23 depleted equivalents.

On 17 September, any remaining hope for an independent Poland was dashed as Soviet forces began crossing into the country along the length of Poland's eastern border. With no foreseeable aid from the West, and left to wither between two military juggernauts, Poland fought on, and attempted to extricate as many men and as much matériel as possible to neutral Hungary and Romania. Soon after the last Polish hold-outs surrendered in early October, a new partition commenced. Germany doubled the size of its rump Upper Silesia province, greatly expanding East Prussian territory southwards, and incorporated the 'Polish Corridor' into the Reich. In the east, the Soviets extended Belorussian and Ukrainian SSR's borders up to the new demarcation line that had been designated on 29 September.

On 27 September, Hitler met with OKW to order senior officials to formulate a plan to invade France and the Low Countries as soon as possible. Not surprisingly, they were cautious of such an endeavour, as Germany had applied nearly all of its warmaking capability to achieve victory in the East, and now needed time to rest, refit and resupply. Having rescheduled an invasion of the West from 25 October to 12 November, Hitler went on to call for a series of face-saving weather-related postponements, and eventually cancelled the planned offensive. Germany simply lacked the necessary strength at present to undertake offensive operations so soon after defeating Poland. Postponed again on 10 January 1940, the great German gamble in the West would finally commence four months later.

Instituted on 7 July 1981, the Medal for the War of 1939 was awarded to Polish Army veterans, and other personnel, who defended the country during September and October 1939. On the reverse it listed 'Za Udział w Wojnie Obronnej Ojczyzna' ('For Participation in the Homeland Defence War') with crossed swords. (Public Domain)

BIBLIOGRAPHY

PRIMARY SOURCES

Allgemeine Heeresamt (1939a). *AHA 3011/39 g.K. AHA I b.*
Allgemeine Heeresamt (1939b). *AHA 3102/39 g.K. AHA I b.*
Heereswaffenamt (1938). *Panzerkampfwagen II (2 cm) (Sd. Kfz. 121): Gerätbeschreibung und Bedienungsanleitung zum Fahrgestell, Fahrgestell Nr. 20 000 bis 27 000, Beschreibung.* Berlin: Oberkommando des Heeres.
Heereswaffenamt (1941). *Panzerkampfwagen II Ausf. A bis C und F: Gerätbeschreibung und Bedienungsanleitung zum Aufbau.* Berlin: Oberkommando des Heeres.
Oberkommando des Heeres (1944). *Merkbl. geh. 28/1: Geheim! Zusammenstellung der Explosivstoffgewichte für deutsche Munition (zu H. Dv. 450 Rdnr. 46).*

SECONDARY SOURCES

Jentz, Thomas L. (1996). *Panzertruppen 1: The Complete Guide to the Creation & Combat Employment of Germany's Tank Force, 1933–1942.* Atglen, PA: Schiffer.
Jentz, Thomas L. & Doyle, Hilary Louis (2008). *Panzer Tracts No. 2-1 – Panzerkampfwagen II: Ausf.a/1, a/2, a/3, b, c, A, B, and C – development and production from 1934 to 1940.* Boyds, MD: Panzer Tracts.
Jońca, Adam, Szubański, Rajmund & Tarczyński, Jan (1990). *Wrzesień 1939, Pojazdy Wojska Polskiego 1939 – Barwa i broń* ('September 1939: The Polish Army vehicles: the colour and weapons'). Warsaw: Publishing Transport and Communications.
Komuda, Leszek (1973). *Polski Czołg Lekki 7TP, Typy Broni i Uzbrojenia, nr 21* ('Polish 7TP Light Tank, Types of Weapons and Armaments, No. 21'). Warsaw: Bellona.
Kozłowski, Eugeniusz (1964), *Wojsko Polskie 1936–1939, Próby modernizacji i rozbudowy* ('Polish Army 1936–1939, Trying modernization and expansion'). Warsaw: Wydawnictwo Ministerstwa Obrony Narodowej.
Kucharski, Wacław (1984). *Kawaleria i broń pancerna w doktrynach wojennych 1918–1939* ('Cavalry and Armour in War Doctrine 1918–1939'). Warsaw: Państwowe.
Magnuski, Janusz; Szubański, Rajmund & Ledwoch, Janusz (2009). *7TP vol. 2.* Tank Power, Vol. LXXVIII. Warsaw: Wydawnictwo Militaria.

Nawrocki, Antoni (1992). *2. Batalion Pancerny: Żurawica 1935–1939*. Pruszków: Ajaks.

Niehorster, Leo W.G. (1990). *Mechanized Army and Waffen-SS Units (1st September 1939)*. Hanover: self-published.

Pionnier, Magdalena (1972). *Charakterystyka zawartości zespołów akt dowództwo – Broni Pancernych, Łączności i Saperów z lat 1929–1939*
('Characteristics of Command – Armoured, Communications, and Engineers from 1929–1939'). Warsaw: Military Archives Service Bulletin No. 4, Central Military Archives.

Schaub, Oskar (1957). *Aus der Geschichte Panzer Grenadier Regiment 12 (SR 12)*. Bergisch Gladbach: self-published.

Seeckt, Generaloberst Hans von (1933). *Deutschland zwischen West und Ost* ('Germany: Between West and East'). Hamburg: Hanseatische Verlaganstalt.

Sultanbekov, Bulat (2005). 'Kama on the Volga'. *Scientific Documentary Magazine*, Issue 2, 2005: 36–39.

Szubanski, Raymond (1989). *Polska broń pancerna 1939* ('Polish Armour in 1939'). Warsaw: Bellona.

US Army (1939). *The German Campaign in Poland 1939*. Army Pamphlet No. 20-255. Fort Leavenworth, KS: CARL.

Captured 7TPs and a C7P (at left). The 7TP lacks its main armament. Note the *Balkenkreuz* has thin white outlines around the white cross. (Courtesy Sergey Ryijov, beutepanzer.ru (Vasily Diounov))

INTERVIEW TRANSCRIPTS

Mieczysław Słupski, Tactical-Reconnaissance Officer, 2nd LTB (late 1939, France).
Julian Świątkiewicz, Doctor, 2nd LTB (26 October 1945, Germany).
Mieczysław Bielski, OG Piotrków (Warszawa: Wydawnictwo Bellona, 1991).
Jan Karpiński AA Platoon, HQ/2nd LTB (9 December 1945, Italy).
Konstantego Hajdenki, Commander, 2/2nd LTB (27 November 1939).
Mieczysław Białkiewicz (1943, Iraq).
Józef Rejman, Commander, 3/2nd LTB (29 September 1951, London).
Aleksander Kruciński, Technical-Logistics Company, 2nd LTB (no date/location).

Vickers E Type As during manoeuvres near East Prussia. Although the original photograph caption states it was taken on 1 April 1939, the depicted 'Japanese-style' camouflage had been replaced on all Polish tanks after 1936/37, during which time the external, four-digit vehicle numbers were removed. The white triangle on the hull is a tactical symbol for 2nd Platoon. (Haynes Archive/Popperfoto/Getty Images)

INDEX

Figures in **bold** refer to illustrations.